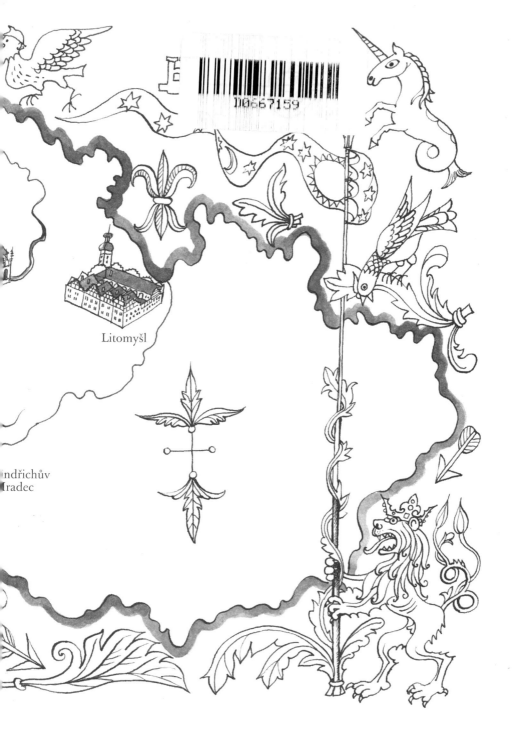

Litomyšl

ndřichův
Hradec

# 22 Czech Legends

alena ježková

# 22

# CZECH
# LEGENDS

**PRÁH**

The Czech lands have long been a region of tales and legends. Indeed, every Czech castle, manor house or medieval town has its own apocryphal history, long preserved in the memories of the common folk and written down by many an anonymous chronicler across the ages.

Legends and myths have a special magic, standing between the two worlds of fantasy and reality. They fill the dry facts of history with a tinge of poetry, humour, and even hope, understandable to all with ears to hear.

# Český Krumlov

## I. The Founding of Krumlov Castle

On the place where the town of Český Krumlov now stands, there once lay in ages long past nothing but deep black forests. They were the home of many wild animals, even lynxes and wolves hunting in fearsome packs, and were said to keep secret in their depths many places of dangerous enchantment. Through these woods ran the primary trading route from Austria into the fertile valleys of central Bohemia. A greater threat to travellers than any of the wild denizens of the wood, though, was a band of fierce robbers, whose lair was hidden in a high cliff not far from the ford across the river Vltava. These bandits would attack wealthy merchants, horsemen, even the poorest of travellers without exception, steal all their property, and then leave them dead or lamed for life.

The raids of the bandits were put to an end only by one courageous South Bohemian squire of the name of Vítek. With a picked body of men, he set out to fight the robbers, and in a bloody struggle finally killed them down to the last man. Then, on the site of the former robbers' lair, Vítek ordered the construction of the fortified castle Krumlov. And on the river banks below the castle, a town soon began to grow. Its oldest street, Latrán, is said to bear its name from the Czech word for bandit – *lotr*- in memory of the suffering that they once caused.

But this story is only a legend. Historians assert that the name is derived from the Latin word 'latus', which means 'side', and simply indicates the side street leading along the castle ramparts into the old medieval quarter.

# II. The Dividing of the Rose

One of the most famous treasures on display in the palace in Krumlov is the historic painting entitled "Dividing the Rose". It depicts the old heraldic legend that tells of how Lord Vítek of South Bohemia divided his property among his sons. Though in the present telling of the legend the names of the sons are taken from renowned members of the line born at later times, it is nonetheless true that the founder of the noble house, Lord Vítek (?–1194), is a real historical figure. With tireless efforts, he expanded and improved the lands of his South Bohemian estate. He ordered the clearing of forests and the creation of fields and pastures, mended the roads and built fords across the rivers, and built stalwart castles. At the end of his life, he was the ruler of the entire southern part of Bohemia. And, it was said, not even the king could match the number of men-at-arms who could be summoned under the family standard of the five-leafed rose.

Lord Vítek raised his sons well, leading them to great skill on the field of battle and in the management of their estates. Yet when they were full-grown, he long refused to yield his rule to any one of them. Only when he had completed the impressive castle of Rožmberk and moved into it did he finally begin to think of what would happen once he was gone. Already, he was much advanced in years, and spent entire days wrapped in mantles of heavy fur mantles before the hearth in the castle hall.

One day, he called for his youngest (and his favourite) son, Vok, to be brought to him.

"Summon to Rožmberk all of your brothers, Vok. I would like to divide among you, in all true justice, all that I have brought together in my lifetime. Yet each one of you will be responsible for his own share of the estates, and this will be made clear by the division in our family

shield. Henceforth, order the making of shields and pennants each with a rose of a different colour: one gold, one white, one blue, one red and one black!"

Vok promised his father that he would do as he had asked.

"Yet if I may, Father, ask but one question – why have you divided the rose of our house into five colours? After all, there are only four brothers…"

Lord Vítek only smiled mysteriously.

"My son, the answer shall be known once all of your brothers are gathered together."

In a few weeks, the sons met again at Rožmberk Castle. Lord Vítek called them into the grand banqueting hall, and also called for his seneschal Sezima to be summoned. Then he spoke to each of them:

"Jindřich, unto you I entrust the lands around the town of Hradec. Your shield shall be, from this day on, a gold rose on a field of blue. To you, Vilém, I entrust the land between Landštejn Castle and the city of Třeboň and the arms of a white rose on a red field. As for you, Smil, you shall rule under the sign of a blue rose on a field of gold, and your estates will be those of Nové Hrady, Stráž nad Nežárkou and Bystřici. And for you, Vok, unto you are granted the castles of Rožmberk and Krumlov, and the old family arms of a red rose on a white field".

Then the sons received from their father's hands the new shields and pennants.

Still unclaimed, however, was the banner and the shield with a black rose on a field of gold.

"Now it is your turn to approach, Sezima," the aged lord ccalled to his seneschal. "Up to now, you have never been told that you are also a son of mine, even if born to a mother of common stock. I, however, believe that the strength of every family is in its descendents. For long years have you served me, without ever knowing me to be your father, and so you too are deserving of your share. You shall rule in Ústí under the black rose".

Sezima was struck with surprise at his lord's words, yet equally was deeply touched. He kissed his father's hand, and embraced his half-brothers.

Shortly thereafter, Lord Vítek died. The glory and the power of his line, known after him as the house of Vítkovec, still remains with us. For centuries, the many-coloured roses bloomed on the shields and the banners of his descendents, and later were assumed into their heraldic insignia by many a South Bohemian town.

# III. The White Lady of Krumlov

The ghostly manifestation of a lady clad all in white is a peculiarity of the family of the lords of Rožmberk. Legends are related of her appearing in all of the castles of this noble house – at Český Krumlov, Rožmberk, Jindřichův Hradec and Třeboň. An actual basis for the tales of the White Lady is the historic personality of Lady Perchta z Rožmberka (1429-1476).

The beautiful daughter of Lord Oldřich of the Krumlov branch of the Rožmberks, she is said to have spent a happy childhood in the castle of Český Krumlov. When she grew to womanhood, many highly-born noblemen contested for her hand in marriage. However, in that age, the groom was invariably chosen by the father, and the daughter had no choice but to obey. Marriages among the nobility of medieval and Renaissance times were almost never a question of love, but exclusively the advantageous joining of noble families, properties, and political power.

A single meeting between Perchta and her future husband Jan z Lichtenštejna was enough to convince the young noblewoman that she never could love him. He was a widower, a man of birth and power to be sure, yet in his character harsh and wounding. His heart was of stone. The unhappy girl pleaded with her father to betroth her to another, yet Lord Oldřich would hear nothing of the kind. Soon the house of Rožmberk was celebrating the wedding festivities, and immediately after, the lord of Lichtenštejn took Perchta away, to the Moravian chateau of Mikulov.

Delicate and refined to the very marrow of her bones, Lady Perchta found the life to come an endless time of sorrow and suffering. In the Mikulov chateau of the Lichtenštejn family, there also lived the lord's mother and the sister of his first wife, who turned her life into as great a torment as they possibly could. And the lord of Lichtenštejn not only watched them passively, but added his own share of cruelty and

heartlessness to the mix. All in vain did Perchta write again and again letters of despair to her father and then her brother, begging them to free her from this hell. Yet they did not help: in this age, it was unimaginable that a woman would ever leave her husband, however cruelly he might treat her.

Only after many long years did Perchta's sorrows come to an end, with the death of her husband. It is said that on his deathbed, he begged for her forgiveness, as he felt burdened by his conscience. Yet she refused to forgive him – and at that moment, the tale continues, the lord of Lichtenštejn cursed her for eternity.

As a widow, Lady Perchta returned to her native castle of Krumlov. The people knew her as a tall, slender, prematurely aged lady with a grave face, who never smiled. Yet since she had undergone such cruel trials and sorrows herself, her heart was full of compassion for all who suffered. She always helped as best she could, and never turned away a person in need.

When she died, quite soon the lords and ladies of the house of Rožmberk began to see her figure walking through the corridors of the family's castles, always robed in pure white and with a sorrowful face, just as in her lifetime. Even after her departure from this world, she was thought to be looking after her relations, and informing them of events to come. Black gloves on her hands, for instance, told of misfortune or death. She greatly liked the small children born into the family. Whenever she heard, during the long nights, the crying of infants whose nurses had fallen asleep above the cradles, she would go to them, take the babies in her arms, and comfort them herself. The old family retainers knew her well, and never interfered with her. It was said that the White Lady particularly loved the last son of the Rožmberk line, little Petr Vok.

Once, though, a new nurse was brought in to care for the children, one who knew nothing of Lady Perchta. When she saw one night a vague white form bending over the cradle to caress the little boy, she shouted:

"What are you doing here? Put the child down at once …!"

Lady Perchta turned towards her, and answered angrily:

"This child is more mine than yours! You should take care to perform your duties with greater diligence, and not to leave infants to cry by themselves!" Then she came over to the nurse, petrified with fear, and added: "Never more shall I appear, so you must take care of the child yourself. But when the boy grows up, tell him how I loved him. And show him the place where I took leave of his cradle."

After these words, the White Lady walked over to one of the walls and disappeared into it.

From that time on, she has never been seen at the castle of Krumlov. However, the nurse could not forget the meeting, and when Petr Vok reached manhood, she told him what the White Lady had asked. Petr Vok then ordered an examination of the wall where the White Lady had disappeared, and when the workmen had broken through it, found behind it an enormous treasure of gold.

Still, not all of the legends of the White Lady date back to the depths of history. It is still said that she appeared in the castle of Rožmberku in the year 1944. Then, under the tragic occupation of the Czech lands by the troops of Nazi Germany, the castle was the home to a training camp for members of a Nazi women's organisation. One morning, two girls climbed up to the tower, to hang a swastika flag from it as usual. At a great height above the tower, they saw hovering in the air a transparent female form in a white gown, who stared angrily at them. Almost out of their minds with fear, they called for their commander, at whom the White Lady shook her fist and then vanished. The entire case was instantly subjected to investigation by the Gestapo, convinced that it must be a provocation by local residents, yet the appearance of the White Lady was never logically explained. The two girls, however, lost their minds shortly after their sighting of the spectre and never recovered.

The last incident in which a report of the White Lady was recorded happened at Rožmberk in 1996. During that year, the castle was undergoing extensive restoration, and on nearly all sides was surrounded by scaffolding. One of the painters, at work in one room on the first floor, ssaw, beyond the window, the figure of a woman in a white veil walking back and forth outside. At first, he believed that a trespasser was climbing along the scaffolding, yet he suddenly recalled with horror that on that one side of the castle, the scaffolding had been removed. When he leaned out of the window, the phantom of the White Lady slowly dissolved before his very eyes...

Perhaps the White Lady is still guarding the patrimony of the Rožmberk family even today. And since she never threatens or harms anyone, let us believe that she is satisfied.

# IV. The Eternal Rose of the House of Rožmberk

Lord Vilém z Rožmberka (1535–1592) ranked among the leading Czech noblemen of his time. At a mere 16 years of age, he assumed the stewardship of his family property. His primary residence was the castle of Český Krumlov, which he had rebuilt at great expense into a splendid Renaissance palace. Holding the office of the Supreme Burgrave of Prague, he was also active in the diplomatic services of Emperor Maximilian II and Emperor Rudolf II Habsburg. A full four times did he marry, yet none of his betrothals brought him any issue. Thus, after his death, the holding of the property descended to his younger brother, Petr Vok z Rožmberka.

At Lord Vilém's court in Krumlov lived and worked many alchemists, botanists, astrologers, doctors and fortune-tellers. Of this number, several were true scientists, yet a still greater quantity were frauds and fakers, exactly as was true at the court of Emperor Rudolf II in Prague. And they too gave their promises that they would transform base metals into gold, miraculously expand the Rožmberk property, or ensure the lord immortality.

Among this company lived one man, greatly advanced in years. None could recall precisely where he was from, or when he had arrived at the palace, and in turn he spoke to none and requested nothing of them. He was given a tiny chamber beside the stables, where he spent all his days. It was said that he never ate nor slept, but merely read from dust-covered tomes or performed magical experiments. One day, a small boy from the village below ventured to speak to him. The son of one of the farmhands, he would always – whenever he had no work at hand – wander through the castle to unearth its secrets. And so he found his way to the half-forgotten chamber. He turned the handle, and stood in the open doorway.

There was little to be seen in the room: only a table, a chair, and piles of books interspersed with various beakers and retorts. The old man was sitting at the table. He looked up from his book and called for the boy to come inside.

"What is your name?" he asked.

"Jacob, my lord," the boy responded. "And you – are you really a wizard …?"

"I wouldn't say that myself," the old man laughed. "Really, I'm more of a searcher."

"And for what are you searching?"

The old man cast his gaze at the wooden cross that hung on the wall.

"I search for the way. The way that leads back to the origins of everything. I believe that along this way I will find myself and I too shall understand all… Hard to understand, isn't it?"

The boy nodded. He had no idea of what the old man spoke. Yet he was pleased that he spoke pleasantly and made no attempt to drive him away.

"If you would like, come again tomorrow, and you can help me a bit with cleaning. Would you like to?"

Jacob did. And so he soon was coming every day, helping the old man to rinse the glass beakers, arrange the books, sweep out the dust. While he was working, the old man would gladly answer whatever questions happened to spring to Jacob's mind. They talked about life and death, about the human mind and the human soul, about joy and about suffering.

Many years passed. Jacob grew to be a man, and his own mind grew from the conversations with his aged friend. Much there was that he came to understand later, and that he had never comprehended at the beginning, and his own view of the world began to change.

After the death of Vilém z Rožmberka, he was followed in Krumlov by his younger brother Petr Vok. He did not remain long: the castle came

under the power of another nobleman, and the new lord Vok settled in
Třeboň. With the new lord came a new retinue of servants, and many of
the old ones left the castle altogether.

"Soon, I believe, I too shall go," the old man one day told Jacob.
"I feel myself to be near the end of my path. I now know whence I come
and whither I go."

Jacob grew sad.

"No, do not mourn for me. Many other reasons for sorrow still remain. This very day, Lord Petr Vok has died in Třeboň, the very last blossom of the rose of Rožmberk." Then the old man turned his eyes to the wooden cross upon the wall, and said no more for the entire evening.

The very next day, Jacob hurried to see the aged searcher, yet the doors of his chamber were locked from inside. He summoned the blacksmith, and when they had finally broken the lock, they saw that the room was completely empty. Nothing at all remained – not the man, not even his books, not even his alchemical beakers. All that could be seen was an old wooden cross affixed to the wall, and at his centre grew a splendid rose in full bloom.

"He has been transformed" gasped Jacob. "Just look at that rose – nothing like that was ever here before!"

The smith stared at Jacob strangely. He also must be mad, he thought to himself as he removed the cross from the wall. For he could see no rose at all.

"Why it's nothing but an ordinary wood cross," the smith answered. "If you want, take it, so at least you have something to remember your friend!"

A few days later, the sad news arrived from Třeboň to Krumlov of the death of Lord Vok. The old man had been right. The rose of Rožmberk had folded forever, yet this amazing blossom still continues to shine in the memory of history and legend.

# V. The Unfortunate Evelina

The Baroque theatre in the chateau of Český Krumlov is now unique in the entire world. All of its original fittings survive – its Baroque stage-sets and decorations, its precious costumes and props, even the texts and musical scores of the plays and musical scores once performed there. And also with us still today is the romantic tale of how the love-lorn maiden Evelina took her final exit from life on the very boards of its stage.

At the time when the lords of the manor had come to enjoy theatrical presentations in their own residence, Český Krumlov was visited by one widely renowned company of travelling players. The actors were accommodated in the buildings inside the castle courtyard, and the entire palace resounded with their merrymaking. In the hours of the morning and the afternoon, they practiced their roles, and in the evening dispersed to the inns of the town. And at the same time, the players soon came to know each other, since their manager had taken on several new actors for the important performances in the castle.

The manager had a daughter of the name of Evelina. Her youth, and her lovely golden hair, fitted her perfectly for the role of an innocent maiden or a princess. Yet in the new production, her father assigned her the role of a girl who tragically chooses death out of unrequited love. Assuming the role of her lover was one of the new actors, a young man named David. The success of the play depended vitally on the mastery of the roles assigned to Evelina and David, and thus the manager took great pains to ensure that in any free moments the two would rehearse their scenes or repeat their dialogues.

And so the inevitable took place. Young Evelina fell in love with David. She told him nothing of her love; only her acting grew ever more and more convincing. When they attempted the concluding scene, when

Evelina in despair stabs herself with a dagger, all the assembled actors burst into applause and swore that a great stage career lay open for her. The manager was more than satisfied. And David? He knew nothing. Or rather, if indeed he suspected the truth, he did not let on. He was an upstanding young man, and greatly proud of his own acting talents.

Finally the grand evening arrived. In the seats of the castle theatre, there slowly gathered the exalted guests, lords and ladies in the most wondrous garments, adorned with precious stones. Soon, the only guest for whom they were waiting was the lord of the Krumlov estates himself. Evelina and David, already arrayed in their costumes and greasepaint, gazed through an opening in the curtain into the stalls and watched the spectators. So long had Evelina kept her feelings back, at that moment they erupted from her heart like a woodland spring:

"David... I know that I love you, and will never cease to! Tell me nothing but that you love me as well, and that you will take me as your wife ...!"

David froze in terror. He could see that Evelina was speaking in dead earnest. Her cheeks seemed as if on fire, and her eyes sparkled with unshed tears.

"But, Evelina, but..." he sighed. "I already have my bride; we are already betrothed and as soon as I return from Krumlov we are to be wed ...!"

At that moment the fanfare was sounded that announced the arrival of the lord of Krumlov. There was no time to say anything more. The curtain rose, and the two young actors were at once absorbed in the story of the drama. And Evelina acted as never before. At the moments when she was required to weep, real tears coursed down her cheeks; when she was to kiss her beloved, she kissed with her eyes closed. The spectators were entranced. When the first act came to an end, the lord of the manor himself rose from his seat and with long applause called the young pair of actors back out onto the stage.

The manager was beside himself with joy. Already he saw before him a generous award from the lord of the manor, and a future of glory. David, however, merely smiled an embarrassed smile and Evelina stood as if struck lifeless. Immediately, she vanished from sight and appeared only when the second act was to start. Once again, both actors performed as if their lives depended on it. And the tragic ending approached. With bated breath, the audience followed the fate of the unfortunate maiden whose beloved had deserted her, and who had resolved to take her own life.

"I can live no longer", Evelina declaimed from the stage. "Better death than the empty days without his love!" She grabbed the dagger and plunged it into her heart. The blood welled up from her chest, and the girl fell to the stage.

"David," she whispered, and breathed her last.

At once the audience trembled – the blood was actually real…!

The manager gasped in horror, and ran to his daughter's lifeless corpse. Only later did he realise what had occurred. Evelina had secretly exchanged the tin stage dagger for a real blade and – precisely like the heroine of the play – chose death for her unrequited love.

Never could the blood be removed from the floorboards of the castle theatre, however hard the cleaners scrubbed. For many years to come, they say, it remained as a recollection of the despairing love of the beautiful actress.

# *Hluboká*

## VI. The Legend of Execution Meadow

When King Václav II ascended the throne of Bohemia, following the death of his father Přemysl Otakar II, "the king of iron and gold", he was only twelve years old.

His chief advisor and the regent of the kingdom became Záviš z Falkenštejna, a powerful and wealthy lord from the South Bohemian noble house of Vítkovec. With equal skills on the field of battle and in the council chamber, he brought the kingdom to further strength and prosperity. And, through marriage to the widowed queen Kunhuta, the mother of Václav, Záviš became the stepfather of the youthful king. He had great prominence and extensive power, and it seemed that nothing could ever pose a threat to him.

Yet Kunhuta died tragically young, and crushed by his burden of sorrow, Záviš decided for a time to leave the royal court. He left Prague for his castle of Svojanov in the Bohemian-Moravian highlands. Shortly thereafter, though, he married again and not long afterward fathered a son. Once again, his life blossomed with renewed joy, and Záviš yearned to share it with his former protégé. He ordered his horse to be saddled and set off with his retinue to Prague Castle, to invite Václav to the christening ceremony.

At the royal court, however, much had changed in the intervening time. A coterie of nobles had carefully intrigued their way into the king's favour; they strongly disliked the lord of Falkenštejn and hoped to destroy his position and his power. For a long time, they had striven to persuade the young king that Záviš intended to seize the throne for himself, until the king himself believed their words. Once Václav was informed that Záviš was on his way, he issued orders detailing how he was to be received.

The lord of Falkenštejn arrived with a light heart, pleased at the thought of seeing the court and the king after such a long absence. In the courtyard of Prague Castle, he leapt from his horse, and hurried to the palace.

His way, though, was soon blocked by the royal chamberlain.

"Good health to you, chamberlain. I have come for the king – is he in his palace?"

"My greetings to you, Lord Záviš. His royal majesty is today not receiving any visitors".

"The knights of Falkenštejn may come to the king at any time," Záviš answered with a frown. "Stand aside and let me pass!"

The chamberlain, however, remained where he was, with mockery in his eyes. All at once, as if from nowhere, the royal guard appeared with drawn swords. Lord Záviš finally understood what had happened. Treachery!

"You are a captive of his majesty, Lord Záviš," said the royal chamberlain. "Once his majesty the king desires to receive you, he will explain himself what your misdeeds have been!"

Many days did the lord of Falkenštejn spend in the dark dungeon, until finally the guards escorted him from his cell and brought him in front of the king.

King Václav gazed down at his prisoner, whom his guards had forced to kneel at his feet. His former friend, advisor, and the wedded husband

of his deceased mother knelt before him, emaciated, filthy, in tattered rags and his hands in fetters.

"Falkenštejn," spoke the king, "you and your house of Vítkovec hold the castles that from time immemorial have been the property of the crown. You have gained them dishonestly. Hence it is my decision that you shall remain my prisoner as long as your family refuses to return its castles to the rightful royal ownership!"

"That is a blasphemous lie, your majesty!" shouted Záviš. "Who has whispered this slander into your ear? You know as well as I that we have paid honestly and fully for these castles to the royal treasury …!"

The king merely waved his hand, and Záviš was dragged back to his cell.

The other lords of the house of Vítkovec soon learned of Záviš's imprisonment, yet there was nothing they could do to help. As for discussions with the king, he absolutely refused to hear their petitions. For two years, King Václav held Záviš in his dungeons, and in return for his freedom demanded all of the castles of the Vítkovec family. And for two years, Záviš repeatedly refused. Then, the king sent his soldiers to lead Záviš in chains around the kingdom, demanding the surrender of the castles for the sparing of the life of the lord of Falkenštejn. Several castles in fact surrendered under this threat.

In August of the year 1290, the sad procession made its way to the castle of Hluboká, where the burgrave was Záviš's brother Vítek. By then, the much-tormented Záviš could hardly remain standing. In the meadow below the castle, the royal herald once more proclaimed the king's command.

"His majesty the king demands that you surrender the castle. Otherwise, Falkenštejn shall be instantly executed!"

Vítek's heart was wrenched at the sight of his brother in chains. Yet he could not sully the honour of his family by confessing to a crime that had never been committed, even to save his brother's life.

"I shall not surrender my castle. The house of Vítkovec gained it honestly, and paid the king for it in full!"

Vítek watched from the ramparts as the executioner drew the sword from its sheath. Two serfs rolled out the wooden block, and the soldiers

raised Záviš to his knees. The blade flashed in the sunlight, and below the blue sky of August, the head of Lord Záviš fell to the ground.

On the spot where the noble blood of the lord of Falkenštejn was shed, for many years – so the legend runs – only red grass would grow. Today, all that remains is the name "Execution Meadow" for the field beside the much later chateau at Hluboká.

# Jindřichův Hradec

## VII. The White Lady of Hradec

When Lord Adam (1494–1531) assumed the ownership of the estate of Jindřichův Hradec, the manorial holding was deeply indebted, and there was no question that increasing the splendour of the castle had to wait for the future. However, Lord Adam proved his worth through faithful service to King Ferdinand of Habsburg, who in turn rewarded him with great munificence. Under his reign, Lord Adam of Hradec ranked among the eight richest men of the kingdom. And then he could start with the grandiose and costly rebuilding of his residence. The most valuable part of the entire building work was to be the gigantic Hall of Gold, large enough to be entered on horseback or even serve for the holding of tournaments.

Yet from the very beginning, the work was plagued with ill fortune. The masons and the labourers saw in this misfortune the hand of diabolical forces, and feared to continue. When the wife of Lord Adam, the kind-hearted Lady Anna, heard of this, she herself came out among the builders and encouraged them to work:

"Fear not and work hard! If the work finds its results, my husband will give you a generous reward."

Many indeed found her words encouraging. Yet there were others who answered her thus:

"Easy enough to say, my lady. But how are we to work when our stomachs are tortured with hunger …?"

Instead of answering, the lady of the manor commanded that a thick soup be prepared, and all who were hungry received a full bowl and a slice of bread.

"Nor is this all," promised the Lady Anna. "If the building is completed in time, every one of you will receive an entire roasted fish, soup, bread and sweet porridge!"

Imagine – if the work is completed well, Lady Anna will prepare us all a feast! murmured the workmen among themselves. With the vision of such a promise before them, the stones flowed from beneath their hands like a miracle. And the tale of the promised feast quickly spread around the entire lands of the estate.

"Have you gone quite mad?" complained Lord Adam when he heard of his wife's promise. "The thought of you feeding that lazy rabble! A hard knout is what they need to get them on the move, not more over-feeding."

Lady Anna stared back hard at her husband.

"If you wish your people to work well, you should not save at their expense! And the food and the sweet porridge I plan to cook myself. Or would you like it to be said that the lady of Hradec cannot keep her word …?"

Lord Adam merely slammed shut the door of his chambers.

From that moment on, the building work continued at such a pace that one could hardly believe it. Stone-cutters shaped the frames of windows and doors, carpenters and wood-carvers were hard at work on the ornamented wooden ceilings, and on the smooth walls, painters brought forth wonderful frescoes. Lady Anna often went among them, telling them what was not to her liking, and praising them when their work had been done well. All the craftsmen were pleased to see her, and each of them recalled to himself her astonishing promise.

By Easter, the entire project was complete. On Maundy Thurs-

day, Lady Anna called up to the manor house all who had worked on its embellishment, as well as the most destitute paupers from the surrounding vicinity. The lord of Jindřichův Hradec grew furious at the thought of how much it would cost. And yet, when he heard from the mouths of other noblemen words of praise for his generosity, he was flattered, and without a complaint paid for everything.

Then, Lady Anna made her way to the dark kitchen in the depths of the castle. She called for a full net of fish to be brought in from the Vajgar Pond, set boiling a cauldron of thick soup, ordered the baking of loaves of fine, thin-crusted bread. And in the end, she herself cooked the porridge, and sweetened it with honey so generously that the porridge itself turned a golden colour.

On Maundy Thursday itself, the castle of Jindřichův Hradec appeared almost under siege from the hordes of the poor or the simply curious. Even those who did not suffer from hunger made their way to its doors merely to see the lady of the manor as she acted as servant to others. And Lady Anna was ashamed of nothing. For every one who came, she served up the food and added a tender smile. From early morning until evening, she distributed food to all and sundry, and even ordered another cauldron of soup to be cooked so that everyone could have his rightful share.

Quite soon, Lord Adam grew convinced that good deeds lead to good rewards. He even grew proud of the generous heart of his spouse, and in his will left a legacy to ensure that all the future lords of Hradec would have the funds to cook sweet porridge for the poor on Maundy Thursday in her memory.

When the Lady Anna finally slipped the bounds of this earth, she was mourned by the poor of all the lands around. And yet the lady of the manor did not completely leave her earthly home. Not too long afterwards, she began to be seen in the castle: in a long white dress, with a veil around her head, and a bunch of keys to the castle doors at

**36**

her waist, just as she wore during her lifetime. At first, the people feared her. Yet when they realised that she would not do them any harm, they began to greet the apparition politely, and she responded with a slight nod. With inaudible footsteps, she walked along the corridors, the folds of her white dress flapping as if in a high wind, only the faint tinkle of her keys announcing her presence. By observing the expression on her face, people learned how to predict future events. If she was smiling, it meant the coming of joy or the birth of a child from her line; if she was weeping or lamenting, it invariably meant that tragedy had struck.

After many years, the lord of Jindřichův Hradec became one Lord Jáchym. He was a man of wealth, but perhaps too economical. Very quickly, he calculated how much the yearly serving of sweet porridge for the poor was costing him. And so, one year just before Easter he let it be known that no porridge was to be prepared at the castle. Soon, many of his people who had seen the White Lady and held her in high esteem came to Lord Jáchym in all faith to implore that he not disrupt the age-old custom.

But Lord Jáchym only shouted in response: "No ghost is going to issue me orders! Whoever believes in the White Lady can go on believing in her. I have my own mind. No porridge is to be cooked, and this is my final word!"

The people merely shrugged their shoulders and left him to his own devices.

That year on Maundy Thursday, the gates of the castle remained firmly shut. It was treated as a day like any other. Yet when that night Lord Jáchym lay himself down to sleep in his bed of the finest goose-feathers, he was awakened by a tremendous noise. The doors of the chambers opened by themselves only to close with a crash; iron pots went rolling around the kitchen, and chairs flew backwards and broke into

splinters. Horrified, the servants ran all around the castle: "The Lady of Hradec is clearly angry!"

But Lord Jáchym had no desire to believe them. He ordered his carriage to be readied, and went to spend the rest of the night in an inn in the town. On the second day, however, everything was repeated, and the same was true for the third and the fourth days. After all this, Lord Jáchym was finally convinced of the truth of his servants' beliefs and invited all the poor of the countryside to the castle for sweet porridge. As soon as he had done so, he had peace. Yet never did the White Lady actually appear to him, until much later.

Lord Jáchym lived to a great age. When he was already quite advanced in years, one night he was struck with such weakness that he could not even call to his servants to assist him. He lay in the darkness of his own bedroom, and felt that his last hour was approaching. All of a sudden, he heard a faint tinkling of keys, and right at his bedside noticed a white female form. Her dress was flapping as if in a wind, and her face was as white as winter ice. And she was staring fixedly at him.

The Lady of Hradec! In deadly fear of her, Lord Jáchym raised his hand, yet no word could he utter. And then the White Lady vanished.

Not far from the castle, at the Jesuit seminary, Father Mikuláš Pistorius was at that very moment deep in his theological studies when he was disturbed by a quiet knocking. When he opened the door, he saw in the corridor the White Lady. She nodded to him to follow her. The priest could not say whether he was awake or dreaming, yet he left the seminary and followed the apparition right to the castle gates. There, the White Lady disappeared. When he told the guard beside the gates what had happened, he instantly let him inside.

The priest was already aware that something serious had happened to Lord Jáchym. He hurried to his chamber. When he entered, he noticed a cluster of weeping relatives surrounding his bed. At his arrival, they looked up in wonderment: "But we completely forgot to send for you, Father! How could you have known that Lord Jáchym was dying…?"

Father Mikuláš did not stop to answer them. He bent over the dying man and granted him the sacrament of extreme unction. Only once Lord Jáchym had peacefully breathed his last did he tell the assembled relatives who had led him to this bedside.

And from this time on, all of the lords of Hradec have taken the utmost care not to say an unjust word concerning the White Lady. They always treated her seriously, and held her legacy in the highest esteem.

# VIII. How Absolution Was Granted For Wine-Drinking

When knighthood was in flower, it was the custom to display one's fortitude not merely in battle, but even in the hall of banqueting. The length of the feasts, the quality of the delicacies served, even the expense of the table utensils were all testaments to a ruler's standing. And the strength of the knights themselves was measured by how much drink they could hold.

Much the same held true for the feasts given by Lord Oldřich z Hradce at his castle in Jindřichův Hradec. And yet, the pious Lord Oldřich, who held the highly prestigious office of the royal server at the court in Prague, knew very well from his years as a courtier where an excess of food – and still more of drink – could lead. Intoxication often loosened tongues, and words were cast that would never have been uttered in sobriety. From here, it was only a step to fights, brawls, and even duels to the very death.

Lord Oldřich z Hradce thus long meditated on how best to bring his feasts to an end in good time, yet not to appear impolite or to invite the slander that he was a miser. And in the end, he hit upon a very clever solution. When the lords had come to his castle for a friendly evening, once the food had been devoured and the servants had for some time merely been filling the goblets, the lord of Jindřichův Hradec called for a dish of plain boiled peas to be brought forth. Then he rose from his chair, tasted the peas, and drained the last of his wine in a toast to his neighbour at the festive board in honour of the Last Supper of Jesus. Following his example, the others did the same. And no more wine was poured, and the feast came to its ceremonial end. Other nobles found this habit to their liking, and many of them also instituted it at their own courts. And as legend states, news of this practice

among the estates of Bohemia came to the ears of the pope himself, who is thought to have decreed that every Czech nobleman who ends his feasts in this way will receive absolution for the length of forty days. In other words, the lords would be forgiven of all the sins that they had committed in the forty days beforehand.

As a result, this custom remained in force for many long years in Bohemia, and all concerned were unsparing in their praise. Only the nobility from across the borders felt a deep envy for the Czech nobles – who could imagine that God's mercy could be won simply by feasting and the enjoyment of good wine …?

# *Karlovy Vary*

## IX. How Karlovy Vary Was Founded

The hunt and the chase were always ranked among the favourite amusements of Europe's crowned heads of past ages. In this matter, King of Bohemia and Holy Roman Emperor Charles IV was no exception. It was his pleasure to go hunting both close by his court in Prague, in the forests of Křivoklát and Karlštejn, as well as in more distant corners of his realm, wherever royal affairs of state happened to lead him. Once it so transpired that King Charles and his retinue happened to visit the castle of Loket at the foot of the Ore Mountains. When the assembled host had settled all necessary matters, the king was pleased to accept the invitation to set forth on the hunt.

They rode out at the very break of dawn. Yet they had no luck, as if their quarry knew precisely to avoid them. The hounds pressed their noses to the ground in vain for the traces of a herd of stags or roe-deer, nor could the sharp eyes of the royal huntsmen catch sight of anything. It was almost at the prick of noon when there suddenly emerged before the huntsmen an impressive stag of sixteen hands in height. Its splendid antlers rose from its head like a crown, and its massive body was covered with shining fur.

"This is a quarry fit for a king …!" shouted Charles and spurred his horse onward after the stag. Already, he was dashing away through the thick undergrowth. The huntsmen loosed the hounds and ran them-

selves towards their prey. Yet the stag seemed to have magical powers: the crackling of the branches that broke beneath his powerful torso came suddenly from one side, then from the other. The horsemen raced their steeds over deep ravines, the stony beds of streams, into the darkest thickets of the virgin forest.

All at once, the stag mounted a high cliff falling sharply down into the valley below. Before the hounds could catch up to him, with a gigantic leap he cast himself into the abyss and vanished. The dogs were hot upon his traces, yet very soon the riders heard only their forlorn howls at the foot of the cliff. From high above, the participants in the hunt searched for their quarry, but a pale fog had arisen from the valley and nothing could be seen. And so they had to turn their horses around, dismount, and carefully descend along the narrow cliff-face. All the while, they could not but hear the howling and moaning of the hounds, rising from somewhere not far from the river.

When they had descended to the valley, they saw a sight of greatest wonderment. Amid clouds of steam, a spring of boiling water was spouting from the bowels of the earth and flowing onto the ground. Lying in the water were the unfortunate hounds, painfully scalded by the water's heat.

"What an amazing spot …!" announced King Charles. "Much have I heard of similar springs in foreign lands, springs whose water is said to have curative properties. This could be one of them!"

Having long suffered from painful ills of the joints, the curious emperor immediately desired to test the healing powers of the hot water. As soon as he had bathed in it, he immediately felt a physical relief. And shortly after this incident, in the year 1350, Charles IV founded beside the spring the town that now bears his name – Carlsbad, or as we now know it, Karlovy Vary.

The precise spot where the imperial and royal sovereign first bathed in the healing waters was, according to the old tales, precisely where the town hall now stands. And the steep cliff where the miraculous stag made his final jump is even today called Jelení skok – Stag Leap.

# X. How the Wedding Party Was Turned to Stone

In the deep valley of the river Ohře, between the towns of Loket and Karlovy Vary, there rises a series of striking rock formations known as the Svatoš Cliffs. Ever since the 19<sup>th</sup> century, they have been a favourite destination for excursions by guests of the spa. During one stay in Karlovy Vary, they were even visited and sketched by the great German poet J. W. Goethe. Linked to these cliffs is the ancient tale of Jan Svatoš and the wedding party turned to stone, which was later used as the basis for the opera *Hans Heiling* by the German composer Heinrich Marschner.

As the tale goes, in one nearby village there once lived a wealthy farmer who had a daughter of the name of Eliška. When she had reached the age suitable for marriage, she fell in love with the young stone-mason Arnold. Indeed, they formed a beautiful couple – Arnold was a strapping swarthy youth, while Eliška had a milk-white complexion and hair as gold as fresh-cut grain. Her heartfelt love had only one flaw: the stonecutter Arnold was as poor as a churchmouse, and Eliška was the bride of the richest farmstead of the vicinity.

Every evening, the lovers met in secret in a clump of trees at the bank of the Ohře. Hidden among the long branches of the willows, they would embrace and talk of their future together. Yet their love seemed, at this moment, more of a rose-tinted dream that could never be brought fully to earth.

One evening, though Arnold made a firm decision: "We can no longer go on like this. Eliška, I shall ask your father for your hand in marriage."

"But you know that my father will never accept you as my bridegroom…" answered Eliška as her eyes filled with tears.

"Don't cry, I've planned everything. I know that your father will refuse my suit. But I also plan to say to him that I shall leave for the city, and there I shall earn such a fortune that I can bring you back to a new farm of my own."

Eliška was saddened, but knew that Arnold's plan was a good one.

"Three years will suffice for me. All I wish to hear is that you will wait for me faithfully. Will you do so …?"

Eliška promised that she would.

The next day, Arnold went to Eliška's father and explained his plans to him. He was a wise man, for he knew that nothing could prevent love from arising in the hearts of the young, and he also liked the honest Arnold. So he answered:

"If this is what you have agreed with Eliška, then it is agreed. Come again in three years, and we shall see if you deserve my daughter's hand!"

Very soon after, Arnold set off. The waters of the Ohře flowed onwards for weeks and months, then for an entire year and after it a second year. Eliška waited, yet no news came of Arnold.

However, there also arrived in the village another man, who had left it long ago. He had travelled the entire world, grown wealthy, and decided that he would finally settle in his native land. His name was Jan Svatoš. Across the village, strange tales were told of him; there were even whisperings that his prosperity was the work of Satan himself. Jan Svatoš nonetheless soon became friends with the rich farmer. Frequently, he paid him visits and related him many a yarn of his travels around the globe, of long sea voyages, of the strange customs in distant kingdoms. The old farmer greatly liked his stories, and soon began to feel lonely when Svatoš did not stop by. And he became aware that he never arrived on Fridays – instead, he would always lock himself for the entire day inside his house, not even answering when neighbours knocked.

The farmer grew curious, and so he once asked what Svatoš did every Friday in his home.

"What it is," answered Svatoš, "is that a promise of mine forces me to spend every Friday alone, repeating my prayers."

The explanation seemed clear to the farmer, and he asked no more.

Eliška, though, did not like Jan Svatoš one bit. She could hardly say why, yet felt a sense of evil and danger emanating from him. And so she was terrified to the very marrow of her bones when her father confided in her that Svatoš had asked to marry her.

"For heaven's sake, father …! You remember, don't you, that I'm waiting for Arnold!" she shouted.

"Have no fears, my child," the farmer said. "I have told Svatoš that you shall give him an answer yourself!"

Eliška feared the moment when she had to speak with Svatoš. Yet when it actually came to pass, it seemed that Jan Svatoš accepted his refusal reasonably. He did, however, extract from the farmer the one promise that if Arnold did not return in his promised three years, he would become Eliška's husband.

From that moment on, Eliška did not sleep a single night, and during the day wandered around the farmstead like a ghost. She had good reason to fear – for the third year was slowly coming to its end, and Arnold nowhere to be found. Every day, she ran out to a nearby meadow, where the road to the village could be clearly seen, and spend hours at a time waiting for her beloved. And on the very last day of the three years, she finally saw her hopes fulfilled: she saw her very own Arnold returning in a procession of several men on horseback, clad in wonderful garments. She rushed from the meadow like the wind, came running to meet him, and collapsed with joy in his arms.

Arnold's companions watched the long-delayed meeting of the lovers with much sentiment. When they had come back to their senses, they began to talk one over the other. Eliška revealed what would have hap-

**48**

pened if Arnold had returned only a few days later. One old man at the head of the procession took notice of the name that Eliška mentioned:

"Did you really say Jan Svatoš, my child...? Why, we know him well!"

The others agreed with fear in their voices.

"You can hardly know what a terrible fate you have escaped! He is a true villain, in league with the devil himself. In our city, he wrought much evil, and had to flee from justice... But let's go for now, we can deal with this rascal later!"

When Eliška had led to her father's farm Arnold and his retinue of richly caparisoned gentlemen, the old man could hardly believe his eyes. Arnold greeted him politely and said:

"I have come just as I promised. For three years I worked hard, and became a rich man. I ask you now for the hand of your daughter Eliška!"

"And I and my associates have arrived with Arnold to testify that everything that he says is the truth," said the oldest man. "I hired Arnold three years ago as a mason on one of my buildings, and he displayed such talents and abilities that he soon became a master craftsman and the most sought-after builder in the vicinity. I would be glad to give my daughter in wedlock to such a man, if only I had one!"

The farmer was touched at this. He gave his blessings to Arnold and Eliška, and then invited all his companions to enjoy a rest after their long journey with good food and drink. Soon, the conversation turned to Jan Svatoš.

"That wretch who was to have been Eliška's husband deserves nothing less than the gallows. We know him all too well …!"

The farmer was taken aback at this news. Yet now he had before him much more welcome worries than the turbulent past of Jan Svatoš. At the urgings of Arnold's travelling companions, he decided to hold the wedding immediately the next day so that they could all take part.

That day was a Friday, the feast-day of St. Lawrence. The entire village was caught up in the celebrations, as the happy farmer invited all its inhabitants. Only the doors of the house of Jan Svatoš remained shut, yet none missed his presence. After the ceremony in the church, the bridal couple made their way to the farmstead. The house beside the resounded with merry-making, which continued deep into the night. It was nearly midnight when the last guests made their departure, and the only ones to remain were the family and their closest friends.

When the church bell had tolled midnight, from out of nowhere a powerful wind sprang up. The wind howled with terrifying shrieks, tore leaves from the trees, and among the terrified wedding party there suddenly appeared Jan Svatoš. His face was distorted into a horrifying grimace as he called out into the whirlwind:

"Devil! I end your service, yet demand of you that you destroy all of these people …!"

"But then you will be mine," a voice emerged from the whirlwind.

"I know it!," answered Svatoš. "I know that I belong to you and expect only the torments of the Abyss …!"

At that moment, from all the hills columns of fire belched forth, and their hot breath transformed all members of the wedding party into high stone cliffs. Just as they were at that moment, so they remained in stone: the groom embracing the bride, while the rest held their hands clasped together in prayer.

"Svatoš," the wind chanted mockingly one last time. "They shall remain blessed in their death, and all eternity is theirs. You, however, are mine, and no trace of you shall remain on this earth …!"

With a single breath, the whirlwind carried Jan Svatoš to a dizzying height, and then cast him downwards into the foaming wave of the river Ohře, which with a ferocious crashing, covered his body for ever.

The next day, the young men and the maidens came to the farm to offer their congratulations to the new couple and give them flowers. Behind them walked the entire village. In horror, they gazed upon the cliffs and saw in them the images of their friends. Weeping, the girls and boys placed their flowers on the cliffs, and promised that they would never forget the tragic story of Arnold and Eliška.

Since that time, young couples in love have made their way to the Svatoš Cliffs to pray for a blessing and protection of their passion. As a custom, it is long gone, yet the legend is told time and time again.

# Karlštejn

## XI. The Devils of Karlštejn

Many were the hosts of strong men who worked on the construction of the castle Karlštejn. Following the plans of the French builder Mathias of Arras, the masons set about first of all with the laying of the foundations and the raising of the walls. Carpenters wielded broad axes to form the thick timber of the roof-beams. Stonecutters assembled the vaulted ceilings from individual stones prepared beforehand, tile-layers covered the roofs with tiles of hard-baked clay, and blacksmiths swung their hammers to create the window-grilles, door-hinges, and covered locks. Still greater in number, though, were the hordes of untrained workmen, carters and day-labourers, who hauled the stones and assembled the scaffolding. In addition to the actual work of building, there was also the crafting of the stone flagging, the windows of stained or painted glass, and the hanging of the walls with sheets of thin-hammered gold and semiprecious stones. Charles IV, King of Bohemia and Holy Roman Emperor, often arrived to ensure that the work was proceeding according to his demands. For hours on end, he would walk around the castle, closely observe the workmen, and ask detailed questions of nearly everyone.

For the time that work was underway on the castle, the workers and the master craftsmen lived in wooden huts that they had constructed themselves beside the road, not far from the ford at the river Berounka.

Along the road ran an unceasing flow of horse-carts bringing building materials, wood, stone, even highly valuable furniture. Yet quite soon the rumour began to spread that at the points where the road narrowed between two cliffs, it was haunted by devils, who were thought to attack the wagons or even solitary travellers, and tear them into shreds.

Soon all the workmen were filled with terror. They began to tell themselves that it was certainly because the very forces of the infernal abyss yearned to disrupt the emperor's magnificent work. And when Charles IV himself heard of these stories, he had it proclaimed that he would give great riches to whomever would bring an end to these devils.

But his knights were afraid. To charge in battle against a hostile army – of course, such is the honour of a knight. But to trifle with the forces of Hades? No one wished to do so. And so no one came rushing to the emperor's aid – until one day there arrived at the court of Charles IV one brave shepherd. He doffed his greasy hat, bowed deeply, and said: "Honoured King and Emperor, I have come to offer you my help. I believe that I can easily take on any of these devils!"

"Excellent", declared the king. "Finally I have found among my subjects one who is so brave that he does not fear the devil himself! Tell me what you shall need, shepherd, and I shall give it all to you."

"Your Majesty, I need nothing too extraordinary. I've already thought it through, and I will need exactly two sacks of dried peas, two horses and one sack of salt." Charles IV was greatly surprised, but he gave the shepherd what he had requested.

That evening, the shepherd salted the peas thoroughly, stuffed them back into the sacks, and placed them atop one of the horses. He mounted the second horse himself, and rode off to the place where the devils were known to live. Just before the entrance to the cliffs, he slapped the horse with the sacks of peas on its back hard on the rump, setting it off down

the road at a brisk trot. As for himself, he hid at the edge of the forest,
where he could keep an eye on what was happening.

When the devils caught the scent of their booty, they crawled out from
their hiding placed in the cliff, and with growling and squealing, threw
themselves onto the sacks of dried peas. There were two of them, and
of quite a fearsome appearance: long curling horns, chicken-claws with
sharp talons instead of hands, eyes glowing fire-red and long tongues
hanging down past their teeth. The devils by now were more than hungry,
the highly salted peas were much to their taste, and they swallowed everything down to the very last pea.

Then one of them sniffed the air:

"Brother," it said, "I think I can smell human blood close by. And since I'm still hungry, I think I'll have a look around. And also – who ever saw a horse travelling without a rider?"

"No, brother," said the other, waving his claw. "I'm no longer hungry myself, instead I feel that I've eaten too much. The peas were much too salty, and I have a ruinous thirst."

The first devil had no desire to remain alone, so both of them leaned down by a filthy pool of water in the road, and gulped it straight down. And then it began: the peas that they had devoured began to swell inside their stomachs. The devils grabbed at their bellies, rolled on the ground and howled with pain, until their stomachs finally burst.

The shepherd rubbed his hands together with satisfaction at the sight, left his hiding place, stripped the devils' bodies of their skin, and rode off to his rude hut, where he fell asleep in good satisfaction.

In the morning, he set off towards Karlštejn to tell King Charles of his deeds.

Bowing politely to the king, he handed him the devil-skins and said:

"Honoured emperor and king, I have destroyed the devils, just as I promised. And now I bring you all that remains of them!"

The king was struck dumbfounded. "You are brave indeed, o shepherd. And fully deserving of my reward. You may have from me the use of an entire manor farm not far from here, where you can raise your sheep as your own master. And whenever I will need someone of great courage, I will have my men call for you!"

The high-born lords and knights at the king's side made all varieties of uncomplimentary faces at this speech, yet King Charles only smiled to himself. If only there were more such shepherds, he thought, my own lords would occasionally have to feel ashamed at their cowardice!

From that time on, no more devils have ever been seen at Karlštejn.

# XII. The Blind Beggar and His Loyal Dog

After the death of Charles IV, the throne descended to his son King Václav IV, Holy Roman Emperor and King of Bohemia. He too appreciated the comfort and the bejewelled halls of the castle Karlštejn, yet he never spent his days there in solitude and meditation, as had been his father's wont. Under Václav, feast followed feast, lordly processions set out to hunt in the Karlštejn forests, and the king himself was ever surrounded by a lively social coterie.

In those days, at the castle gate sat blind Beneš with his loyal dog. Sometimes he would be waiting for the uneaten food from the castle kitchen, at other times he simply warmed himself in the sun and listened to the sounds nearby. His greatest joy, though, was when he was called upon to entertain the king with one of his songs or his versified rhymes, which he composed himself and knew endless numbers. The king and the entire castle staff liked Beneš, and never allowed anyone to take advantage of him.

Once it happened that King Václav was host at Karlštejn to the ruler of one of the German principalities, Prince Bernhard of Braunschweig. His chamberlain was a man of overweening pride and an evil turn of mind. He noticed old Beneš and commenced to mock him: "Hey you, blind old dodderer, wake up and give us a song or two! Why there's no other use to be got from you than to give a bit of fun to your betters, like me!"

Beneš understandably found these words insulting: "I was not brought to this world to serve as a joke. Perhaps a better use for that would be such a proud lord as you yourself!"

The chamberlain was angered at these words, and raised his hand to strike the blind man. But the large black dog that had up to that moment lain quietly at his feet jumped up and snapped at the proud chamberlain's arm. And he, like the poltroon he was, immediately took flight.

That evening, the prince of Braunschweig complained to the king that the dog belonging to the blind man at the castle gates had for no reason at all jumped at his chamberlain. Would it not, after all, prove better to dispose of the beast and chase the beggar away from the royal residence …?

King Václav, though, was a just man:

"My dear prince, your chamberlain has invented a pretty story for himself. I actually saw what transpired, as I happened to look out of the window towards the castle gate. All that occurred is that the dog faithfully protected his master."

Then, the king called for Beneš to be brought to him, so that he could sing several of his new songs at the feast that night. Beneš sang a song that he had composed that very afternoon – a song of the love of a loyal dog for its master.

The chamberlain grimaced with chagrin, but King Václav thanked Beneš, had the servants bring him some food, and invited him to remain a while longer in the warm banqueting hall.

This feast, however, was to end in a tragedy. It so happened that the chamberlain offered his prince a new goblet of wine, and that the prince – in recompense for his earlier accusations – sent the goblet on to Beneš. At that moment, the black dog rose up from the hearth and knocked the goblet from his master's hand. The wine spilled onto the floor, and the dog licked it hastily from the floor until not a single drop was left. In only a short time, he fell to the floor with agonising howls, and very soon was dead.

It was clear to everyone that the wine had been poisoned. And the culprit was easy to spot. It was the chamberlain, who had decided to poison his prince at the castle of Karlštejn, so that the guilt for his evil deed would be ascribed to King Václav.

The prince of Braunschweig was touched by the dog's loyalty, all the more so because he had not only saved the life of his master, but met with

**58**

the death intended for himself. He offered to the sorrowful Beneš that he would lead him to his own realm, where he would be provided with a good living until his death.

The old man was glad to leave with the prince, but he did not go far. When they had only reached Litoměřice, he fell ill and died. The prince then commissioned that a stone column be raised before the church in that town depicting the figures of a blind man and a dog, to recall the loyalty that the canine breed can display. Today, however, there is nothing to be seen of this long-vanished monument.

# XIII. The Wedding at Karlštejn

Most characteristic of war in medieval times were the bloody sieges of enemy castles. The invading armies would attempt to smash through the castle gates, or to surmount the ramparts using long ladders. The defenders of the castle, in turn, showered countless spears and arrows upon the besieging soldiers, poured burning pitch down from the ramparts, and hurled heavy stones from catapults. The forces of the besieger had one great advantage in their access to regular supplies of food; those inside the castle walls were restricted entirely to what they had stored there in times of peace. And thus it often happened that castles would surrender after many months of siege, once their food had run out.

A very similar situation once occurred to the men-at-arms stationed in the castle of Karlštejn. It was during the Hussite wars, in the year 1422, when there arrived at Karlštejn a force of twenty thousand Hussite soldiers from Prague, intent on capturing a castle still loyal to King Sigismund. At first, they hastened in for the attack, yet in short time it became evident that the castle was insurmountable. And so they decided to wait and bring the inhabitants of the castle to the point of starvation.

Months went by, and indeed the supplies inside the besieged castle began to run low. The feast day of the patron saint of Bohemia, St. Wenceslas, was not long off. Both sides agreed that they would not fight on that day. And the Hussites even invited the crown's knights from Karlštejn to their encampment for a celebratory feast.

"This will break their resolve," the Hussites said. "Who could resist a festive board rich in fresh game and excellent wine? They are certainly going hungry already, and when we recall to them what joys of the table we are preparing, they will merely surrender of their own accord …!"

At Karlštejn, though, the men were aware of why they had been invited to the feast. They agreed that they would go, but that they would

pretend that they had already eaten to excess. When they were led to the richly laden tables, the knights of Karlštejn had to restrain themselves from reaching out to the dishes and devouring them at once. But they did so. When the Hussites asked how they were faring inside the castle, they merely choked back their saliva and answered with apparent lightness:

"Doing well, of course, how could it be otherwise? Supplies are enough for another three years, and not even fresh game is absent from our plates."

After the departure of the men of Karlštejn, the Hussite encampment was up in arms.

"Did you hear? Clearly the castle has a secret corridor that they use to gain new supplies. Why, they hardly ate a mouthful! We cannot starve them out this way. Our time is wasted here, and we should simply leave Karlštejn alone!"

But the Hussite commander was intent on remaining – though to assure the men that the siege would not be indefinite, he decided to remain in place until St. Martin's Day.

Inside Karlštejn, however, evil times had truly come. The last of the last remains had been eaten, and for each edible mouthful there were five mouths in wait. And yet the brave defenders decided to keep the legend of their inexhaustible supplies alive still longer. And they sacrificed the very last of what they had – an aged billy-goat.

They sent to the Hussite encampment a messenger, who humbly pleaded for a single day's truce. "There is a wedding to be held at Karlštejn, and we want time for the wedding-feast and a rightful celebration!"

The Hussites consented. The very next day, they watched with envy as the company inside the castle danced to music, how they lifted their beer-tankards, how they promenaded in their finest costumes, while the Hussite soldiers had to wait in their encampment, shivering with cold in their flimsy tents and living off the dull fare of the field kitchen.

Shortly after noon, another messenger arrived from the castle. On a large tray he bore what appeared to be a haunch of venison, and announced:

"The men of Karlštejn send their heartfelt greetings and their thanks that they could celebrate the wedding as it requires. And so they have offered a small gift for the commander – a fresh haunch of venison!"

A haunch of venison! Now, the commander of the Hussites was firmly convinced that they must be a secret corridor supplying the defenders with fresh food. He decided to end the siege of Karlštejn, and when St. Martin's Day had come, all his troops were gone.

Who can say if the Hussites ever learned that there never was any wedding at Karlštejn? That the tankards lifted with such gusto by the men inside held no beer, but only empty air? And that the haunch of venison was from the slaughtered goat, sprinkled with "hairs" scraped off of an old saddle ...?

We shall never know the answer. What is certain, though, is that Karlštejn Castle was saved from the Hussite siege – by an old billy-goat.

# *Konopiště*

## XIV. The Treasury of St. George

St George is one of the very earliest Christian martyrs. A colonel in the Roman army, he was tortured to death for his faith by Emperor Diocletian in the year 303. The best-known legend from his life recalls his fight with a dragon that had taken up residence near the Libyan city of Silené. Every day, the town's citizens had to sacrifice two children to the dragon's appetite, and the victims were chosen by lottery. One day, the lot fell to the daughter of the king of Silené, the lovely princess Cleolinda. George felt sorry for the princess, and promised to save her. He heroically fought the dragon, wounded him with his lance, and then led him back to the city, where he administered the final coup de grace. Out of thankfulness, it is said, a full fifteen thousand citizens of Silené then converted to the Christian faith. According to tradition, St. George is the patron of soldiers, as well as armourers and butchers. And he is also the patron saint of England.

Archduke Franz Ferdinand d'Este, heir to the throne of Austro-Hungary and the owner of Konopiště Castle every since the second half of the 19th century, was a very ambitious man. He yearned to be first in everything. Thousands of deer were slain so that the number of antlers in the castle corridors could reach record numbers. And it was from a similar vain ambition that the St. George Treasury was begun.

Once, the archduke happened to hear that King George V of England

held his namesake and patron in great esteem, and that his collection of objects with the likeness of St. George was the largest in the world. And it occurred to him that he could also start a collection along the same lines, and exceed the size of that held by the English sovereign. It was his plan that he would then invite King George for partridge-shooting at Konopiště and then impress him with his much larger collection. From that point on, the Archduke bought and collected an incredible range of objects depicting the saint. For many a year to come, his collection acquired pipes, coins, weapons, swords, vessels, gravestones, statues and paintings with images of St. George.

Yet Archduke Franz Ferdinand never lived to see his dream realised. During a state visit to Sarajevo on June 28, 1914, he fell at the hands of an assassin. His death served as the inspiration for the hostilities that led to World War One, which led to the re-drawing of the entire map of Europe, and the end of the Hapsburgs as a ruling house.

And the Treasury of St. George? It has its place in the castle museum, where it can be viewed even today by visitors from across the world.

# *Křivoklát*

## XV. The Path of the Nightingales

The future King Charles IV, son of King John of Luxembourg and Eliška Přemyslovna, was brought up in France at the royal court in Paris. He returned to his homeland in 1333 as a youth of seventeen, so that in succession to his father he could take over the rule of the kingdom. It was hardly an easy task – the kingdom of Bohemia had long been neglected, and young Charles had an enormous amount of work awaiting him. Very soon, he was followed by his charming French consort, Queen Blanche de Valois, whose beauty and character soon made her a favourite of the royal court and the ordinary citizens.

Charles worked tirelessly on the rebuilding of deserted castles, re-purchased the royal manor farms, and started the construction of a new palace inside Prague Castle. It soon became clear that he had a much greater talent for the ruling of the kingdom than his frivolously-minded father. When King John of Luxembourg after a time decided to pay a visit to Bohemia, Charles proudly informed him of what he had done there. But praise was not forthcoming, as the king had begun to believe those slanderers who insisted that Charles was plotting to overthrow him and claim the throne for himself. In a fit of anger, he commanded that his son depart with Blanche to the castle of Křivoklát, which he was not to leave without his consent.

Blanche had spent her previous life in the aesthetic splendour and gay

sociability of the court in Paris, surrounded by artistry and beauty. She found it hard to reconcile herself to the silence of Křivoklát, buried deep in nearly impenetrable forests. Yet never did she complain to Charles. She knew how deeply he suffered from his father's ill will, and had no wish to add to his worries. Nonetheless, she wandered through the castle's stone corridors like a body without a soul, pale and bent.

Charles, of course, knew very well of his consort's sorrow. Never was the question far from his thoughts of how to make her happier. One warm summer evening, he was standing by the window of the great hall, gazing into the forested valley. The sun was setting, and its last rays touched the tree-tops with gold, where the birds sang. Blanche was just setting out with her ladies-in-waiting along the path below the castle. She walked there nearly every day, simply to enjoy the birdsong, the scents of the forest, and the evening quiet as it spread across the valley.

And at that very moment it came to Charles what to do to give his wife the greatest joy. He called for all the gamekeepers of the Křivoklát forests, and ordered them to purchase from the bird-sellers all the song-birds that they caught, especially the nightingales. Every few days afterwards, the royal servants released into the thickets below the castle new birds from their wicker cages, until the valley resounded to their songs like the very Garden of Eden.

Blanche blushed with joy when Charles revealed to her that it was for her sake alone that he set the entire forest singing. Could she ever have received a gift more filled with love..?

The nightingales settled in the trees below the castle, and continued to sing there for many a year. And the path below the castle, where the princess enjoyed walking down to the valley, came to be known as the Path of Nightingales.

# XVI. The False Alchemist

At the court of Emperor Rudolf II in Prague there lived many honourable and truthful scholars and artists, yet as well a great quantity of mountebanks and charlatans from all across Europe. One of the latter group was the self-styled alchemist Edward Kelley.

In his native town of Doncaster, his surname was Talbot and he worked as a pharmacist and the town chronicler. For the forging of official documents, he was sentenced to the loss of both ears and expulsion from the town. However, in distant Bohemia nothing was known of his shameful past – and since Kelley wore his hair long, none could even tell that the executioner had done his disfiguring work. Kelley first appeared at the Rudolfine court in the year 1588 with a testimonial from the important Czech nobleman Vilém of Rožmberk. The emperor, however, was distrustful after many encounters with persons of fraudulent intent, and required his new alchemist to undergo a test.

"But of course, your majesty!" Kelley agreed willingly. "It will be an honour for me to convince you in person what amazing results can be obtained from my experiments."

Kelley ordered that a giant wooden chest be brought into the imperial alchemists' workshop, and from it extracted various powders and admixtures and handed them to the emperor. Rudolf then placed them with his own hands into the iron cauldron, and carefully examined each one in turn to make certain that none of them had gold already mixed into them. Then the emperor as well placed the cauldron above the fire, and watched as the flames melted its contents into a glowing red mass. When everything was complete, Kelley left the room, along with the emperor and his servants, carefully locked the door and handed the key to the emperor.

"Here is the key, and order your most loyal guards to stand in front of

the door, to ensure that no one shall enter. I will now call upon all of the assisting spirits to transform the mixture into gold. After one hour, we shall meet here again."

The hour passed in no time. The emperor was afire with curiosity. When they entered into the chamber, nothing had been touched. Only – at the bottom of the cauldron, in place of the molten mixture, shone a grain of true gold …!

Rudolf II was beside himself with joy. He could already imagine how endless streams of gold would start to issue forth from his alchemical laboratory. And he ordered that Kelley receive everything for which he could ask. Kelley, though, only wanted money to purchase secretive and rare ingredients. The emperor was glad to give him the money, and even doubled the promised sum so that the expected gold would be of twice the quantity.

From that moment, Kelley lived in Rudolf's court as the official alchemist, and thoroughly enjoyed all of its delights: splendid garments, good food and drink. Thanks to the emperor's favour, he grew very rich, and was able to purchase the building known as the "Faust House" on the Cattle Market, now King Charles Square (Karlovo náměstí) in Prague.

But the weeks and months went by, and no gold was to be seen. From time to time, the emperor asked with growing unwillingness when it would be completed. And Kelley answered with a falsely apologetic tone:

"Dear emperor, the spirits are not yet prepared for such a great quantity of gold as I wish to make for you. Nor can you know how careful I have to be to entice them, how much effort and strength it costs me...! No, unfortunately we must await the favourable conjunction of the heavenly constellations".

"And when shall it come?" inquired the emperor.

Kelley shrugged his shoulders in embarrassment: "Perhaps in a week, perhaps in a month. The heavenly luminaries are hard for a mere mortal to divine..."

And so more time passed. Yet no tree grows to the heavens, and no lie continues forever. The rumour began to spread around the Rudolfine court that Kelley was a fraud. One of the courtiers even managed to discover how Kelley had cheated the emperor during his trial. The wooden chest in which the servants had brought the precious substances and vessels into the laboratory had a false bottom, where Kelley's brother

**74**

had been hidden. Once the emperor left the room, he replaced the mixture in the pot with gold and once again hid in the chest.

Yet not even these rumours caused as much damage to the false alchemist as his actions when he killed one of the imperial servants in a duel. Finally, Rudolf lost patience. He sent his armed guard for Kelley, yet he had already escaped on a speedy horse. In a short time, however, he was quickly caught and imprisoned in the tower known as "Huderka" in the castle of Křivoklát. There he was to stay until he finally provided the emperor with the secret of the creation of gold, the elixir of life, and the philosopher's stone, as he had so often promised.

Nonetheless, the fraudulent alchemist had no intention of meditating on the secrets of the natural sciences in the darkness of his cell in Huderka. He often gazed out of the window, and in his mind measured and calculated the height of the stone walls. And in secret, he wove from the threads of his own garments and other fabrics a long rope. When one day it seemed of sufficient length, he tied the rope to the window-bars and slipped down the side of the tower along it.

Perhaps at this moment he really did call upon the spirits to help, yet it was in vain. The rope snapped, Kelley fell to the ground and broke his leg so badly that it had to be amputated. Believing this accident to be punishment enough, the emperor released him. For a time afterwards, Kelley continued to wander around Bohemia with a wooden leg, here and there committing some small delinquency for a few coins.

Justice, though, caught up with him in the town of Most, where he was charged with new frauds. Imprisoned there, Kelley took a poison of his own making and brought his life to an end.

# Kutná Hora

## XVII. The Monk and the Silver

As late as the 12<sup>th</sup> century, the place where the town of Kutná Hora now stands was covered with deep forests stretching as far as the eye could see. These lands were the estate of Lord Miroslav z Cimburku, who invited the Cistercian order of monks to clear the forests, plough up the land, and create new settlements. In return for this, he awarded them the right to use the profits from the lands for their own purposes. Most of the monks settled in the village of Sedlec, where in 1142 they created the very first Cistercian monastery in Bohemia.

One monk of the name of Antonín, the hero of our tale, lived in the Sedlec monastery nearly a century later. One warm day in the year 1237, he set off on a stroll through the surrounding woods, having been assigned the task of determining new sites for the clearing of timber and the creation of new arable land. He walked deeper and deeper into the forest, until he reached a cliff-face covered in thick moss. Nearby ran a burbling brook, and fresh green grass shone in the sunlight. Tired from his walk, Antonín decided that the time had come for a rest. Leaning his back against the cliff for comfort, he closed his eyes.

But it was not his lot to have a quiet sleep: instead, he dreamed a most unusual dream. He saw himself setting out into the forest with a mattock to overturn stumps. Hardly had he made a few strikes at the earth, when it rang with a metallic echo, as if his mattock had struck an iron box. He

bent down, removed a few clumps of sod, and before his eyes flashed the glare of silver! Antonín feverishly dug away, and everywhere that the blade of his mattock fell there appeared pieces of silver – silver boulders, even silver tree-roots.

From this dream, the monk awoke in a sweat, and he looked around himself in confusion to see where the silver of his dream had vanished.

And he looked at the cliff above his head – and saw three thick veins of silver running through the rock!

He wiped his eyes, touched the rock, yet the silver did not vanish. It was real.

The monk fell to his knees and thanked God for the miraculous dream that had brought him to wealth. Then he removed his habit, hung it from a tree near the cliff so that the spot would be easy to find, and hurried back to the monastery to tell the brothers of this joyful news.

Not too long after, the monks opened the first silver-mines in the side of the cliff, which attracted many people from both far and near. In a short time, the first miners' camp had risen nearby, which was later built into the rich medieval silver-town now known as Kutná Hora. And its name – literally "Habit Mountain" – is said to have come from the monk's robe that indicated the first finding of silver in the land. However, modern historians tend to believe that the name Kutná Hora comes from the word "kutat", to dig in the earth.

# XVIII. The Gnomes of the Mineshafts

From that moment when the first silver mine was opened not far from the monastery in Sedlec, new mines appeared in the vicinity like mushrooms after a heavy rainfall. In no time at all, nearly every hill and cliff were drilled full of mineshafts striking ever deeper and deeper into the bowels of the earth.

In the underground corridors carved into the living rock, only lighted by the dim flares of smouldering oil lamps, the miners worked. With heavy sledgehammers and iron picks, they knocked the silver ore from the rock and in gigantic baskets carried it up into the daylight. And if the banging of the hammers fell silent for a moment, the miners would often hear, emerging from the depths below, a mysterious knocking and tapping. They knew that these were the good spirits of the silver mountains – the mine-gnomes. These were tiny men with long white beards, no bigger than a cat and slightly smaller than a dog, yet in all other ways quite similar to people. And their garb and tools were hardly any different – appearing in tiny miners' smocks with miniature lanterns and hammers. The miners knew them well – very often, the mine-gnomes would appear to them in the dark tunnels and with their wee fingers show them where they should dig. For their aid, every year the miners gave the gnomes new red cloaks. In the evening, they would leave the garments, prettily ornamented by the miners' wives and adorned with silver buttons, in the tunnels. When in the morning they came back to work, the cloaks were no longer there. Sometimes, though, it happened that the miners did not notice that an entire year had passed, and forgot to reward the gnomes. Then, the gnomes took their revenge, and played various tricks on them – blowing out their lanterns, hiding their hammers, or leading them into side-shafts where they wandered lost for hours at a time.

Old and experienced miners knew that in the placed where the

tapping of the mine-gnomes echoed the loudest, the mineshaft was at greatest danger of flood. But the younger ones often paid no attention, or even mocked them as cowards. It was said that the gnomes were heard day and night in the Šmitna mine in 1509. However, its miners did not take notice of the mine-gnomes' warning and continued with their digging. Very soon, underground water unexpectedly burst into the shaft, and all eighteen miners who happened to be working there were drowned.

# XIX. The Drowning of the "Donkey" Mine

No one knows how the "Donkey" mine received its name, but it was one of Kutná Hora's richest sources of silver, giving forth the ore so generously that it could be excavated without cease for many dozens of years. The miners were greatly proud of the Donkey, and why should they not be – after all, it was the source of their livelihood, as well as the place where they spent the most hours of the day. The oldest among them knew a rhyme that prophesied:

*As long as the Donkey shall roar and bray,*
*Good luck in our fair town shall stay.*

As it happened, a rich supply of the glittering metal was there for several generations of miners. Yet nothing lasts eternally, and the mine was no exception. One day, when a group of miners was digging at its greatest depth, they smashed through a wall of rock behind which, in the hollows of the rock, lay giant lakes of icy water. Unaware of the danger, the miners broke through the rock, and at that moment the water rushed out with terrifying force and washed them away. Eight miners met their deaths in the deepest shaft of the Donkey, and a mere three more were almost miraculously saved.

With the news of the tragedy, alarm spread through the town. The dead were dead, and such tragedies have always belonged to the craft of the mines – but what will happen once the Donkey is flooded …? All with the hands to do so grabbed wooden buckets or leather water-skins and raced to the mine. At the edge of the shaft they erected wind-lasses and started to draw up the water. Day and night they toiled, for several weeks. Yet the work was all in vain, and their hopes a mere fancy. The water rushed ever and ever upwards, without any trouble filled the winding network of mineshafts, as if the people had carefully prepared its

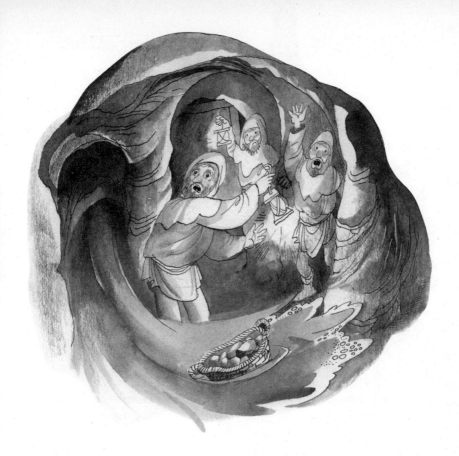

path. There was nothing to do but cease with the rescue efforts and leave the Donkey to its unavoidable fate.

The Donkey, it is said, filled with water for a full fourteen years. By the year 1554, the water began to spill across the edge and the mine was completely drowned.

And the words of the old miners' prediction came true. Hardly had the Donkey ceased to "roar and bray" that the other silver mines in Kutná Hora began to bring forth ever less and les silver, and with every new day came closer to their eventual end.

# *Litomyšl*

## XX. The Haunted Chamber

In the year of 1567, the estate of Litomyšl along with its ancient castle was acquired by Lord Vratislav of Pernštejn. A man of much wealth, he decided to rebuild the grim fortress into a sublime Renaissance chateau. The residence that he created was not merely dazzling but truly a welcoming place to live.

Possibly, though, it was even during the ownership of Vratislav that tongues began to wag in the town that one of the castle's chambers was haunted. Soon it became clear that no one could live or even spend the night in the haunted room. No sooner would the clock strike midnight, in the room terrible sounds began to be heard, along with hollow thumps and scraping as if an invisible being were bumping into the furniture or re-arranging it.

Once there arrived at the chateau one impoverished nobleman and requested a place to sleep. For the lord of the manor, though, the guest did not seem sufficiently elevated, and so he told the butler to assign him the haunted chamber. The nobleman was glad that he had a roof over his head for the night, and hardly had he lain down on the pillow but he was fast asleep. But as soon as midnight had struck, a sound like a thunder-clap rang out directly beside his head. The guest jumped from his blankets and stared in terror into the darkness. All around him he heard scraping and grinding, and he even would have sworn that he heard laboured breathing. He froze in terror – yet because the room was bathed in moonlight, he saw that there was no one in it.

At that moment the room echoed to a deep voice declaiming: "Saecula saeculorum!"

The nobleman waited no longer. Still clad in his dressing-gown, he leapt from the bed and ran into the corridor. He roused the butler and told him his outrage at what a shameful prank he had played. That very night, he left in high dudgeon, and was never again seen at the Litomyšl chateau.

After this incident, the lord of the manor decided to lock the chamber and not allow anyone to enter. He feared that the ghost might actually harm someone. And the servants as well were relieved. In particular, they were glad never to have to clean in the room, since they feared entering it even in the daytime.

Seven years passed after that visit, when one evening a mendicant monk knocked at the manor door. He was given food, and then asked for a bed for the night. The butler, though, shook his head, since no room was free. Then he remembered:

"There is one room unoccupied. But for seven years now, no one has entered it, and it must be horrifyingly dirty."

"This is no problem for me," the monk rejoined. "As you know well, my duty is to serve God and to wander the country. I am used to sleeping in far worse placed than simply a dusty bedchamber!"

"But this one is also haunted," the butler admitted. "If you wish, I shall have it opened. But if anything amiss should happen to you in the night, it is your responsibility and not mine!"

"What ill could befall me?" the monk laughed. "The good Lord is here to protect me from ghosts and all the infernal powers!"

The chamber was indeed far from clean. It corners were hung with spiderwebs, and the furniture covered with a thick layer of dust. But the

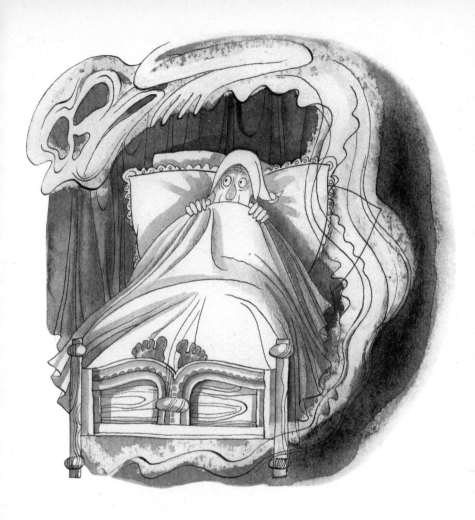

coverlets of finest goose-down were as soft as in past years, and so the monk lay down among them and fell asleep.

At midnight, as happened many years before, the thunder-clap sounded. The monk was instantly awake, crossed himself and fearlessly said to the darkness:

"What do you wish, spirit? If you are suffering from your sins, tell me how I can help!"

A hiss of breath and a wave of cold spread through the room. Then the voice declared: "Saecula saeculorum!"

The monk instantly recognised the Latin phrase from the liturgy of the mass. And he also knew how to answer it:

"Amen!"

The invisible ghost responded with delight: "My thanks to you! I am free!"

This was the last sound from it. The ghost had vanished. And in the deep silence that followed, the monk fell asleep once again.

That morning, the butler knocked on the door of the chamber. When the monk had told him what had happened that night, the butler could hardly express his gratitude sufficiently. He gave the courageous monk food and money for the journey, and set him off with his heartfelt best wishes.

The chamber in the chateau was then thoroughly cleaned and put to use, like all the others. And if there was ever anything more to be heard in the night, it was merely the contented snoring of its sleepers.

# XXI. The Proud Countess

In byegone days, it is said that there lived at the chateau in Litomyšl a very proud countess. From morning to night, she did nothing but change from one set of expensive clothes into another, try on different pieces of jewellery, or torment her unhappy servants. Nothing for her was ever good enough, and all her pieces of clothing or adornment had to be unusual and unique.

So many dresses did she have that they occupied an entire room – red, yellow, green, pink, flowered, striped, of the thickest velvet or shining silk, with gold embroidery, trimmed with fur or swan feathers, pearls, shining glass beads… And as soon as she had worn the dresses once, she never put them on again, since they had already been seen once before.

One day, she was gloomily casting her eye over her wardrobe. At the next estate, they were holding a splendid ball, and she had nothing to wear! She reached for a bite of the delicious cake that she had been brought for a snack – and at that moment had an idea.

"Bring me at once the cook," she ordered her maids.

When the cook in his snow-white apron had arrived, the countess at once told him:

"Bake me a dress. Of the sweetest white batter, fluffy as a feather! Decorated with coloured icing. Have it ready by tomorrow. And watch out not to burn it!"

The cook was terrified at what the countess had ordered him to do. A dress of pastry? Who had ever heard of such a thing? But he dared not defy her, and immediately set to work. He called for a seamstress to come to the kitchen and reveal to him how the fabric for a dress is cut. Then, he baked a flat sponge-cake of the finest white flour, sugar and eggs, and sliced it according to the dress-pattern. And then, he glued the parts together using icing from egg yolks. By now it was evening, and everyone set off for

bed. Only the unfortunate cook had to remain awake through the entire night, decorating the pastry-dress with coloured hearts and roses of marzi-pan, so that it would be ready at the break of dawn.

The countess was greatly pleased with her dress. She was beside herself with joy that she would have something to wear to the ball that no one else would. But the cook and the maidservants took their own view of the matter. Indeed, they were troubled by such a thoughtless act – food is, after all, food and should not be wasted. There would always be more

**91**

than enough of the poor and the starving who would never in their lives enjoy a mouthful of such pastry as that used for the countess's dress.

When evening had fallen, the countess put on her dress of pastry and rushed to her carridge. In the manor courtyard, though, a poor, bent beggar-woman blocked her way.

"Have mercy on me, your honour, my children at home are starving and I have nothing to give them …"

But the countess hardly looked at her. She shouted to her guards:

"Chase that filth from my property!"

The beggar-woman's eyes flashed.

"You squander food for your amusement, but would leave my children to die of starvation? May God strike you dead on the spot …!"

At that moment a thunder-clap rolled from the heavens, the earth split, and the countess fell into a bottomless chasm. The earth closed over her forever. But not even this fate was sufficient punishment for her pride. Quite soon, the ghost of the countess began to appear during the nights in the chateau. Still clad in her bizarre dress, she wandered the corridors searching for one who could free her.

Once a young nobleman was spending the night at the chateau. He awoke in the middle of the night, and found that the ghost of the countess was standing beside his bed. "Help me to find peace after death," she implored him. "Only a young knight such as you can free me from my torments …!"

"And what should I do, my good lady?" the youth asked.

"You must find the beggar-woman whom I refused to help when I was alive. And you must ensure that her family will never suffer from hunger. And one more matter – never tell anyone of me, otherwise misfortune will strike you and I will haunt the chateau forever!"

The terrified youth promised the countess that he would do whatever she said. Immediately, the apparition vanished.

For the rest of the night, the young nobleman could not sleep a wink. At the first cock-crow, he called for his horse to be saddled, to leave this accursed spot as fast as he could. But whether he truly wished to free the unfortunate Countess from her fate, or merely promised so out of fear, no one shall ever know. When the guards at the gate asked him why he was leaving so early, the young man told them of his meeting with the ghost. As soon as he had said the final word, his horse took fright, reared up, and the nobleman fell, breaking his skull on the flagstones of the court-yard. He was dead in an instant.

And as for the ghost of the proud Countess? Most likely, she waits for her liberation even today.

# *Třeboň*

## XXII. The White Horse of Petr Vok

The last of the line of the rich and powerful house of Rožmberk, which for over three centuries held sway in South Bohemia, was Petr Vok (1539–1611). Nearly all of his life was spent in the shadow of his older brother Vilém, who was the ruler of the family estate. For this reason, Lord Vok never gained any influential position or enjoyed political might. He lived in seclusion at the chateau in Bechyně, where he devoted himself to scholarship, literature and art. His private library was said to be one of the largest in Europe, and his collection of artistic works, scientific instruments and natural curiosities bore comparison only with the famed collections of Emperor Rudolf II. After the death of Vilém in 1592, Petr Vok inherited full responsibility for the entire property of the house of Rožmberk. Having no heir of his own, he sold the Krumlov castle in 1601 and settled himself in the chateu of Třeboň.

Lord Vok commanded for all of his collections and artwork to be brought to the Třeboň chateau as well. And when he had taken up residence there, both the chateau and the town came to life again. Visitors and emissaries from distant lands arrived to visit Lord Vok, spectacular celebrations and masked balls were held, and the lord would often tour his estates in the summer in an open carridge, and in winter in a horse-drawn sledge.

Yet for all this, Lord Vok remained just to his subjects. Even though he had great debts himself, he never raised their taxes or subjected them to new ones. For the poor and the helpless, he took greater care than any other nobleman of the time, or indeed any other: every day at 10 o'clock in the morning and 6 o'clock in the evening, food and drink was given to the poor at the chateau. Hence he was loved by the citizens of Třeboň, who tried to meet all of his wishes, even if some of them may have sounded odd to them.

In his stables at Třeboň, Lord Vok raised horses of the finest blood and the greatest beauty – roans, Arab thoroughbreds, dapple-greys, and stallions from the famed Kladruby line. Yet his very favourite was one old white horse.

"My truest friend!" Lord Vok often said of him. When as a young man, he fought as one of the Emperor's generals against the Turks in Hungary, the white horse carried him safe through the fiercest fighting and saved his life. From that moment on, Lord Vok could never be parted from him. While the horse still could bear him, he frequently rode him around his estates, and as both horse and rider grew older, no day passed when Lord Vok at least paid a visit to his stable.

Yet the day came when the inevitable occurred. A stable-boy came running up to the chateau:

"My lord, your white horse is dying! Come at once, so you can see him one last time alive!"

At once, Lord Vok arose from his table and a goblet of his favourite wine, and hurried along behind the stable-boy. The aged horse lay on his side on a heap of straw, breathing with difficulty. Yet he recognised his master at once. He tried to stand, but no longer could. He gave one sorrowful whinney, and Lord Vok – still in his lace-trimmed banquet cloak – knelt down at his side. He stroked the horse's head and mane, whispered into his ears, and never once held back his tears. In a minute, the horse had breathed its last.

Lord Vok gave orders that no one was to touch the body of the horse. He called to the town for Třeboň's three master tanners, and when they arrived, he told them:

"I have work for you. Today, my favourite horse has died. I would like it if you could remove its skin, tan it, and stuff it to make it appear as if he were still alive. If you succeed in this, I will reward you generously!"

The tanners were struck dumbfounded, since none of them had ever done anything of the kind. Yet they dared not refuse – nor did they wish to, since they held Lord Vok in the highest esteem. "My lord, we shall meet your wishes as best we are able," they promised, and hurried to the manor stables at once. But when the horse-butcher began carefully to strip the skin from the dead horse, they were faced with a grave problem. The horse, being much advanced in age, had skin that was already starting to crack, and the hairs from the mane and tail were hardly holding fast to their places. There was no doubt that no mortal efforts could make this sorry nag into the handsome steed that Lord Vok desired. "Would that the devil himself made quick work of this," spoke the first tanner.

"Speak of the devil only as a last resort – once Lord Vok sees fit to punish us for our poor work. No way around this, as sure as I'm alive," said the second.

"Do not despair, my brethren," answered the third. "I think I know a way out of this fiendish conundrum!"

When he had spoken to the other two, they were overjoyed. Yes, this is how it should be done! And they fell to their task with gusto.

Before a week had passed, in one of the tanners' workshops stood a white horse, as if it were alive. It had a skeleton of wood, was stuffed with horse-hair, and had eyes of glass. And the tanners had even blackened its hoofs and braided its tail and mane with red ribbons, as in the horse's lifetime.

Then they loaded the horse onto a wagon and brought it to the chateau.

Lord Vok ran out to meet them full of expectation. At first, he walked around the horse without a word, carefully touched its mane, sides, hoofs. And then said, his voice trembling, "Masters, you have indeed performed an amazing work. Why, my horse not only looks as if he were alive, but even younger than I remember!"

Then Lord Vok paid the tanners their promised reward, and installed the stuffed horse in his own chambers.

The tanners heaved a sigh of relief. Only they would ever know that in place of the skin of the old horse, they had stuffed the skin of a completely different animal which they had secretly found themselves …!

After Lord Vok died, the stuffed horse was sold at auction, and vanished to whereabouts unknown. However, its ghost is said to appear at night in the town. Several citizens of Třeboň claim to have seen it silently galloping from the chateau through the streets to the workshop of the tanner who stuffed it, and then vanishing. And there are those who say it can be seen even today.

# Table of Contents:

**Český Krumlov**
I. The Founding of Krumlov Castle  /  7
II. The Dividing of the Rose  /  9
III. The White Lady of Krumlov  /  12
IV. The Eternal Rose of the House of Rosenberg  /  18
V. The Unfortunate Evelina  /  22

**Hluboká**
VI. The Legend of Execution Meadow  /  27

**Jindřichův Hradec**
VII. The White Lady of Hradec  /  33
VIII. How Absolution Was Granted for Wine-Drinking  /  40

**Karlovy Vary**
IX. How Karlovy Vary Was Founded  /  43
X. How Wedding Party Was Turned to Stone  /  46

**Karlštejn**
XI. The Devils of Karlštejn  /  53
XII. The Blind Beggar and his Loyal Dog  /  57
XIII. The Wedding at Karlštejn  /  60

**100**

**Konopiště**
XIV. The Treasury of St. George / 65

**Křivoklát**
XV. The Path of the Nightingales / 69
XVI. The False Alchemist / 72

**Kutná Hora**
XVII. The Monk and the Silver / 77
XVIII. The Gnomes of the Mineshafts / 80
XIX. The Drowning of the Donkey Mine / 82

**Litomyšl**
XX. The Haunted Chamber / 85
XXI. The Proud Countess / 90

**Třeboň**
XXII. Petr Vok and His White Horse / 95

**101**

The publication of the volume *22 Czech Legends* was made possible thanks to the financial support of the following:

Regional Government of Central Bohemia

Regional Government of South Bohemia

The Region of South Bohemia

Town of Litomyšl

Town of Kutná Hora

Town of Hluboká nad Vltavou

Alena Ježková
# 22 Czech Legends

Translated from the Czech by Martin Tharp;
Association of Translators and Interpreters - www.inter.cz
Illustrations and cover design by Zdenka Krejčová.
Typesetting by Vladimír Vyskočil - Koršach.
Printed by Ekon, Jihlava.
Published by Práh, P. O. Box 46, 158 00 Praha 5,
www.prah.cz, in 2007 as its 253th publication.
First edition.

# RIVERBED

*David Wagoner*

# RIVERBED

*Indiana University Press*

*Bloomington / London*

SECOND PRINTING 1972

Copyright © 1972 by Indiana University Press

Published in Canada by Fitzhenry & Whiteside Limited, Don Mills, Ontario

Library of Congress catalog card number: 74–166118

ISBN: 0–253–17475–9

Manufactured in the United States of America

For Patt, *who has been there,*
*and here, with love*

# Acknowledgments

The poems *The Fisherman's Wife* (1969), *For a Man Who Died in his Sleep* (1971), *The Gathering of the Loons* (1971), *The Trail Horse* (1971), and *The Makers of Rain* (1971) appeared originally in THE NEW YORKER. The poems *A Victorian Idyll* (1969), *Doors* (1969), *Gift Wrapping* (1969), *Talking Back* (1969), *The Keepers* (1970), and *The Survivor* (1971) appeared originally in SATURDAY REVIEW. The poems *Epitaph for a Ladies' Man* (1969), *In the Badlands* (1969), *The Floating Lady* (1969), and *Last Words of the Human Fly* (1970) appeared originally in HARPER'S. The poems *Fortuna Imperatrix Mundi* (1969), *Riverbed* (1971), *Lost* (1971), *Old Man, Old Man* (1971), and *Fog* (1971) appeared originally in POETRY. The poems *To Be Sung on the Water* (1969), *Song Off Key* (1969), and *Laughter in the Dark* (1970) appeared originally in TRIQUARTERLY. The poems *A Morning on the Outside* (1970) and *The Vacation* (1970) appeared originally in NORTHWEST REVIEW. The poems *The Inexhaustible Hat* (1970) and *The Middle of Nowhere* (1970) appeared originally in SHENANDOAH. The poems *Lying Awake in a Bed Once Slept in by Grover Cleveland* (1970) and *Trying to Think by a Steel Mill* (1971) appeared originally in THE IOWA REVIEW. The poem *The Extraordinary Production of Eggs from the Mouth* (1970) appeared originally in THE NEW REPUBLIC. The poems *One More for the Rain* (1970) and *The Break of Day* (1971) appeared originally in MADEMOISELLE. The poem *The First Law of Motion* (1970) appeared originally in INSIDE OUTER SPACE: NEW POEMS OF THE SPACE AGE, ed. Robert Vas Dias (New York: Doubleday Anchor Books, 1970). The poem *The Doves of Merida* (1971) appeared originally in THE SOUTHERN REVIEW. The poem *The Other Side of the Mountain* (1971) appeared originally in THE AMERICAN SCHOLAR. The poem *A Police Manual* (1970) appeared originally in ANTAEUS. The poems *Do Not Proceed Beyond This Point Without a Guide* (1970) and *The Death and Resurrection of the Birds* (1970) appeared originally in SALMAGUNDI. The poems *Halcyon Days* (1971), *Waiting with the Snowy Owls* (1971), and *One Ear to the Ground* (1971) appeared originally in KAYAK. The poem *A Touch of the Mother* (1971) appeared originally in PEBBLE. The poems *Doing Time* (1971), *Contemplating a Bust of William Jennings Bryan* (1971), and *The Ascent of the Carpenter Ants* (1971) appeared originally in HEARSE. The poem *Elegy for the Nondescript* (1971) appeared originally in THE SENECA REVIEW.

# Contents

Riverbed   1

The Fisherman's Wife   3

The Keepers   4

In the Badlands   6

Talking Back   7

The Trail Horse   8

The Death and Resurrection of the Birds   10

The Ascent of the Carpenter Ants   11

Doors   12

Trying to Think by a Steel Mill   13

A Touch of the Mother   14

For a Man Who Died in His Sleep   16

Song Offkey   17

Lying Awake in a Bed Once Slept in by Grover Cleveland   18

Contemplating a Bust of William Jennings Bryan   20

The Inexhaustible Hat   21

Laughter in the Dark   22

The Extraordinary Production of Eggs from the Mouth   23

Epitaph for a Ladies' Man   24

A Victorian Idyll   25

Six for Sax   26

A Police Manual   30

Fortuna Imperatrix Mundi   33

The Middle of Nowhere   35

Job's Answer   37

One Ear to the Ground   47

Waiting with the Snowy Owls   48

*To Be Sung on the Water*  49
*Halcyon Days*  50
*Elegy for the Nondescript*  51
*The Survivor*  52
*One More for the Rain*  53
*The Break of Day*  54
*A Morning on the Outside*  55
*Gift Wrapping*  57
*Last Words of the Human Fly*  58
*The Vacation*  59
*Do Not Proceed Beyond This Point Without a Guide*  61
*The Other Side of the Mountain*  62
*Doing Time*  65
*The First Law of Motion*  66
*The Floating Lady*  68
*The Makers of Rain*  69
*The Doves of Merida*  70
*The Gathering of the Loons*  73
*Old Man, Old Man*  74
*Lost*  75
*Fog*  76

RIVERBED

1

Through the salt mouth of the river
They come past the dangling mesh of gillnets
And the purse-mouthed seines, past the fishermen's last strands
By quarter-light where the beheaded herring
Spiral against the tide, seeing the shadowy others
Hold still, then slash, then rise to the surface, racked
And disappearing—now deepening slowly
In the flat mercurial calm of the pulp mills, groping
Half clear at last and rising like the stones below them
Through swifter and swifter water, the salmon returning
By night or morning in the white rush from the mountains,
Hunting, in the thresh and welter of creek mouths
And shifting channels, the one true holding place.

Out of our smoke and clangor, these miles uphill,
We come back to find them, to wait at their nesting hollows
With the same unreasoning hope.

2

We walk on round stones, all flawlessly bedded,
Where water drags the cracked dome of the sky
Downstream a foot at a glance, to falter there
Like caught leaves, quivering over the sprint
Of the current, the dashing of surfaces.

In a month of rain, the water will rise above
Where we stand on a curving shelf below an island—
The blue daylight scattered and the leaves
All castaways like us for a season.

The river turns its stones like a nesting bird
From hollow to hollow. Now gulls and ravens
Turn to the salmon stranded among branches.

They lie in the clear shallows, the barely dead,
While some still beat their flanks white for the spawning,
And we lie down all day beside them.

When she said, "No,"
I freed the hook, holding the two-foot rainbow
With both hands over the dock-side in the water.
Its mouth would scarcely move
Though I scooped it, belly down, below the surface
Again and again to rouse it.
Hoping too soon, I let it go. It tilted,
Beginning to slide out of sight, its tailfin stiff.

Again, she said, "No." Before I could take her place,
She had stepped casually in her summer dress
Into the lake and under, catching the trout
And coming upward, cradling it in her arms.
Then breathing less than it, not shutting her eyes,
She settled slowly under water, her face
As calm as that water deep below the cedars.

I caught her by the hair, bringing her back
Alive. The trout slid loose, its red-and-silver side
Flashing beyond her, down into the dark.
I saw the tail flick once before it faded.

I helped her up. She stared at me, then the water.
We sat on edge till the moon came out, but nothing
Rose, belly up, to mock it at our feet.

The drizzle and wind had driven the keepers
Indoors at the marine aquarium.
We stood between the seals and the whale tank,
Our games rained out like theirs.

But she climbed to the round catwalk
Ahead of me, and there was the sleek half-grown
Black-and-white killer whale, being heaved
And lapped by its own backwash.

I couldn't have closed my arms
Around its head, and wouldn't have dreamed
Of trying. It swam in a flat circle,
Surging, as though pacing a cage.

At the opposite side she knelt, held out her hand
Over the gray water, and called
Something I couldn't hear in the wind.
The whale went there and lifted its dark head

And opened its mouth a foot below
As wide as a window. From among the glistening
Perfectly pointed teeth there came
A thick blunt tongue as pink as a mollusc's foot.

She kissed it, as God is my witness. The whale
Sank back and swam as it had before.
She came toward me at the top of the stair,
As I braced against the wind blowing between us,

And offered me those same lips to be kissed.
And something I hadn't dared
Believe in, something deep as my salt
Rose to the surface of my mouth to touch them.

When we fell apart in the Badlands and lay still
As naked as sunlight
On the level claybed among the broken buttes,
We were ready for nothing—
The end of the day or the end of our quick breathing,
The abolishment of hearts—
And saw in the sky a dozen vultures sailing
With our love as the pivot.
They had come in our honor, invited by what could pass
In their reckoning
For the thresh and crux and sprawled languor of death,
Too much pale skin
In that burning bed where we lay at our own banquet,
Being taken in
As thoroughly as the fossils under us
When they lay down;
And the sea that once was there welled up in our eyes
For the sake of the sun.

## Talking Back

This green-and-red, yellow-naped Amazon parrot, Pythagoras,
Is the master of our kitchen table. *Every good boy*
*Does fine!* he shouts, hanging upside down, and *Pieces of eight*
*And gold doubloons!* in his cage whose latches he picked with ease
Till we bought a padlock, *To market, to market, to buy a fat pig!*
*Home again, home again,* and he rings his brass bell, as militant
As salvation, or knocks his trapeze like a punching bag with his
  beak
Or outfakes and ripostes the treacherous cluster of measuring
  spoons
Which he pretends are out for his blood. How many times
Have I wished him back in his jungle? Instead, he brings it here
Daily with a voice like sawgrass in raucous counterpoint
To after-work traffic, washing machines, or electric razors
As he jangles back at motors in general, *Who knows*
*What evil lurks in the hearts of men?* but then, inscrutably,
Refusing to laugh like The Shadow. When he walks on the table
In a fantailed pigeon-toed shuffling strut, getting a taste
Of formica with his leathery tongue, he challenges me
Each morning to fight for my wife if I dare to come near her,
Ruffling his neck and hunching, beak open, his amber eyes
Contracting to malevolent points. I taught him everything
He knows, practically, *Fair and foul are near of kin!*
Including how to love her as he croons in her soft voice,
*I'm a green bird,* and how to test me for the dialectic hell of it,
*What then? sang Plato's ghost, What then?* as if I knew
The answer which Yeats in his finite wisdom forgot to teach me.

*"If I could get Yeats on a horse, I'd put*
*a new rhythm into English poetry."*

—Ezra Pound

Get on, expecting the worst—a mount like a statue
Or a bucking runaway.
If neither happens, if this bay mare holds still,
Then you're off
The ground, not touching the ground except through her
Four stilted corners
Which now plop up and down as carefully
In the mud by the road
As if those hoofprints behind her were permanent.
You're in the saddle
As she clip-clops up the path on a slack rein,
Her nose leading the way
Under the pine boughs switching like her tail.
Give in. Sit still.
It won't be hard to let her have her head:
It's hers by a neck;
She'll keep it against your geeing, hawing, or whoaing.
This one's been bred
To walk from daybreak to darkness in the mountains
Up trail or down
And will do it without you tomorrow. The apparatus
Cinching and bridling her,
The leather and metal restraints for a prisoner
Who *won't* be convenient,
Who *won't* do what she's told or listen to reason,
Are mostly for show:
For example, take this place you're passing now—

Tall stumps and boulders,
Thirty degrees of slope and a narrow trail—
A time for judgment,
A time for the nice control of cause and effect.
Do you see the flies
Clustered around her eyelids, nipping their salt?
Or the humming wasp
Tossed from her tail to her rump where it sinks in?
Suddenly swivelling
And sliding, jerking tight as a slipknot
And rearing out from under
Arched like a cow and a half humped over the moon,
She leaves you alone,
And you part company on the only terms
Possible: hers being yours—
No straddler of winged horses, no budding centaur,
But a man biting the dust.

Falling asleep, the birds are falling
Down through the last light's thatchwork farther than rain,
Their grace notes dwindling
Into that downy pit where the first bird
Waits to become them in the nest of the night.

Silent and featherless,
Now they are one dark bird in darkness.

Beginning again, the birds are breaking
Upward, new-fledged at daybreak, their clapping wingbeats
Striking the sides of the sun, the singing brilliant
Dust spun loose on the wind from the end to the beginning.

# The Ascent of the Carpenter Ants

They bloomed suddenly in April like a bush in black clusters
High on the garage wall, and for an hour in a frenzy
Half of them nudged and bustled goodbye to the half with wings,
Caressing and swarming, till one by one they rocketed
Sixty feet straight up in the air like berserk hornets.

They'd worked all winter for this as they thoroughfared
Against the grain of the rafters, munching wood
Only to make way for a harvest of spring leaves.
And now those staying behind, like me, saw the starlings
Catch the swift fliers flopping gracelessly over the housetops.

Of the short-lived ones who escape, one in a million
Lights on something rotten enough to live in,
The Exterminator said—wanting to spray everything
Inside and out. But I told him I'd think it over
(And over) under the lucky starlings who waited fat on the wires
In case one more turned up. They stared back, daring
Me to toss up anything hard or bitter enough to move them.

All over town at the first rattle of night
The doors go shut,
Flat hasp over iron staple, bolt into strike,
Or latch into groove;
And locked and double-locked and burglar-chained,
All of them wait
For the worst, or for morning, steady in their frames:
From hinge to lock stile,
From hard head-casing down to the plinth block,
The doors hang still,
One side for knocking and one for hiding away,
One side for love
And one for crying out loud in the long night
To the pounding heart.

## Trying to Think by a Steel Mill

Facing this heavy industry, I try to name the substance
Of what's between us: the barbed wire crowning the gate
Was drawn from the heart of pig iron; men pass through smoke,
Smoking, in sheets of steel they pay for and pay for,
Toward blast furnaces and coke ovens, toward alloys boiling
Red and blue in the open hearth, to the jagged scrap heap.

Suddenly, it strikes me like a part flying out of a machine.
It hits me hard, like something I've heard shouted
To straighten me out: thinking is brittle as cast-iron.
You must cram oxygen through it to burn the impurities,
Then heap it downwind, smoke-stack it up and around
Till it falls on houses and trees in a corrosive dust,

But the trouble with thinking then is it won't stay home,
It walks around and stares at the gray case-hardened rivers,
It won't stay in school or in jail or the hospital, and it won't
Work, and it doesn't look or act like thinking:
It's strictly functional like drop-forged hardware,
But oxygen, breath by breath, comes rusting back at it.

She stands in the hallway, waiting for a sign
Of breath or smoke, but nothing squeaks the floor
Or whispers at the sink or drifts through transoms.
She has shut the house for the night, but not her eyes:

She threads them up the stairs like the eyes of needles,
Taking a stitch or two, but not in time:
This is the time when all her basting ravels,
When hooks slip out of eyes, and seams come open.

She goes to bed like all good girls and boys
And sisters and husbands by the hands of clocks,
Whether or not those hands will hold her off
Or turn her in or turn her luminous.

Now she must stir her life until it's smooth,
Folding the beaten whiteness through and through
Her mind, like a level cupful taking its place
With all the rich ingredients of the night,

But something chills her. The layers of her dream
Sink in the middle, stiffen, and turn cold:
What is it? Shut the door, the delivery men
Come slouching and lounging into her preserves,

And first you must wash them clean with homemade soap,
Caress them, dry them gently with a towel,
Then soak them for hours in wormwood and witch hazel,
They will fall off and give you no more trouble,

And after turning thick at a rolling boil,
They must form a ball when you drop them in cold water,
Screw the lids hard and store them upside down
In your dark cellar, they will last forever,

And now you know the measure of everything:
Your hand is half as wide as it is long,
Around your wrist is half around your neck,
And twice around your neck is around your waist,

And the cows come back for the leather in your shoes,
The sheep come back for the wool in the tossing blankets,
The geese come back for the feathers in the pillow,
And something blue goes in and out the window.

## For a Man Who Died in His Sleep

Once in, he can stay as long as he remembers
To lock the door behind him, being afraid
Of nothing within the ordinary passage
Where he hangs his hat and coat, thinking of bed.

He feels as safe as houses: the predictable ceiling,
The floor at its level best, the walls, the windows
Beyond which the sky, under glass, is slowly streaming
Harmlessly westward with its tricks and shadows,

And going upstairs, he lies down to be soft
In a nest of boxes fitted against the night.
He shuts his lids like theirs and, wrapped like a gift,
Presents himself to sleep, to be opened by daylight.

At first, there is nothing, then something, then everything
Under the doors and over the windowsills
And down the chimney, through the foundation, crawling
From jamb to joist and muttering in the walls,

And he lies tongue-tied under the gaping roof
Through which the weather pours the news of his death:
In sheets and lightning, the broken end of his life
Comes pouring crownfire through the roof of his mouth,

And now he dreams he is dreaming that he knows
His heart's in the right place, safe, beating for good
Against the beams and braces of his house
All the good nights to follow, knocking on wood.

I needed to make music, but look what's coming:
Something offkey, ungainly, with a rat and a bum in it,
A song like a dish of peaches spilled on the floor
With nothing fitting or touching anything else except by flopping
Slice over juice to meet the linoleum.

Who said there should be a song like a split ragbag?
Nobody needs it—a song with a hole in the middle
Through which some garbled, red-wigged, black-faced gag
Is sticking its head to be conked with baseballs, a song
Like all the wrong weather tangling sunshine and blizzards.

A song should have its tail in its mouth like a hoopsnake,
Or come to a neat point like a stack of belongings,
Or link and labor its opposites in a fixed sword-fight.
Who wants a song like a dump where anything comes or goes?
Here come that rat and that bum for no good reason.

# Lying Awake in a Bed Once Slept in by Grover Cleveland

One night, this bed was the Ship of State. It sank
In the middle as deep as its hard slats
Under the burdens of office
Which, pound for pound, were seldom greater,
Sir, than under you. In the midst of panic,
You kept your dignity tight as your fob pocket,
Not throwing your weight around but thinking
Slowly, so slowly they said sometimes
The problems went away while you pondered
Mighty issues, harboring grave doubts.

I picture you that night, on your back
(Giving free sway to your personal corporation)
As if lying in state, with the State
Of New York lying six feet below,
Mulling again the disasters of the body
Politic, making up your mind
After the fact like a teacher grading a newspaper—
Homestead, Haymarket, Pullman, Coxey's Army.

Mr. President, a man like a bed can stand foursquare
For seventy years and have no more
To show for it than a plaque.
Last night, I put myself in your place,
Out flat, my feet jammed at the footboard
Trying to slow things down. Outside,
Beyond a bay window, the same State of New York
(Which had dead bushes and leaves all over it)
Was crawling out from under winter so slowly
I couldn't see it move. Nobody asked me

How to do anything. I wasn't required
To nod or shake. Did the riots happen?
What did I decide? The newpapers haven't come yet,
So I don't know whether we made it through the night.

## Contemplating a Bust of William Jennings Bryan

Your bald pate looms as large as a roc's egg
Out of which hatched those flights of rhetoric
Which carried my grandfathers off—Republicans
To a man—almost persuading them
To let go of their rocky principles.
But they held on. High talk was a daily feature
From the bottom of the barrel-chested orotund
Booming local masters of rodomontade
And classic flourishes, when all loudspeakers
And idiot boards were human. In the end,
Jerusalem and Chautauqua were nice cities,
But Ohio was a state of mind,
So they went back to work, shuffling and mumbling.

When they made you, they broke the mold,
And the lost wax went up in smoke
And fire like a well-aimed peroration,
Then on to its reward. And here you are
With your bronze lapels, your long stiff upper lip,
And your pupils like bulletholes—the silver-tongued
Orator who stampeded one convention
But banked on others, including the Bible.
Your tongue isn't showing,
But since you believed in the invisible
Investments of a lifetime, maybe it's there
Like a silver dollar stuck in the wrong slot.

The incomparable Monsieur Hartz in 1880
Without assistants, with only three small tables
On a well-lit stage produced from a borrowed hat
Seven glass lanterns, each with a lighted candle,
A swaddle of scarves, hundreds of yards of bunting,
A lady's bustle, a stack of empty boxes,
A cage with a lovely, stuffed, half-cocked canary,
A life-size babydoll and dozens of goblets,
A shower of playing cards, a gentleman's wig,
And lastly a grinning skull. Oh Monsieur Hartz,
You were right, you were absolutely right! Encore!

# Laughter in the Dark

*For Vladimir Nabokov*

Trying to laugh with our mouths shut is a lesson
In physics, good taste, and raw anatomy;
And since, like titters and giggles, it gets us nowhere,
We might as well let it rip, our throats lying open
Like organpipes, all the way to the belly.
But when we laugh in darkness, we'd better move
Fast, unless we want more company
Than we can use in a dark of our own making,
For soon, over our shoulders,
We'll hear the sinister heart-felt snickering
Of our bent selves, who are no laughing matter.

# The Extraordinary Production of Eggs From the Mouth

As he stands alone on stage, the Professor
Shows us he has nothing
Up his sleeve or under his coattails,
Then lowers his brows as seriously as a man
Thinking of being something else, and there,
Would you believe it, from between his lips
The white tip of an egg comes mooning out.

As softly as a hen, he seems to lay it
In his nested fingers. Another. He eggs us on
To laugh and gag for him, to cluck and crow
For the last things we expected or hoped for—
Eggs in both hands, in tophats and fishbowls—
Till he has so many he could quit forever.

But now with a flick of the wrist, seeming to think
Better of his wobbly bonewhite offspring,
He puts one into his mouth, and another,
And each one vanishes back where it came from
Till all his hatchwork has been laid to rest.
He comes to the footlights, gaping for applause,
And except for the pink, withdrawn, quivering tongue,
We see his mouth is absolutely empty.

His life was dedicated to the proposition.
Girls were his charity, and he gave till it hurt.
Whatever he did to himself was second nature.
First nature now is treating him like dirt.

# A Victorian Idyll

"*A gentleman always falls behind his wife in entering the drawing room. . . . If (the butler) does not know them by sight, he asks whichever is nearest to him, 'What name please?' And whichever one is asked answers, 'Mr. and Mrs. Lake.'*"

—Emily Post, *Etiquette*, p. 350

She came through the room like an answer in long division,
At the top of her form, trailing a dividend.
And when her husband fell down, as he always does,
Flat on his face behind her and met the rug
Like an old friend, we simply sharpened our charcoal.
When the quizzical-looking butler said, "What name, please?"
Someone said wearily, "Mr. and Mrs. Lake."
It's always like this. A few included him
In their sketches as an ambiguous portion
Of the water, but the rest got down to business,
Draping white samite over her rich shoulders
And drawing the sword from their imaginations.

1

*"My God! How horrible!" I exclaimed, and glanced appre-*
*hensively into the dusky shadows of the room. "What is your*
*theory respecting the creature—what shape, what color—?"*
*   "It is something that moves rapidly and silently. I will*
*venture no more at present, but I think it works in the dark."*

—Sax Rohmer, *The Insidious Dr. Fu-Manchu*

Working in the dark regardless of shape or color,
We lose respect, no matter how silently
We take new theories like glancing blows.
We venture at present only from room to room,
Misapprehending God's dear horrified creatures
Who keep pace with our shadows and exclaim,
"Good night, sweet footprints!" over our tingling shoulders.

2

*"How could anyone get into his room?"*
*"I cannot imagine. But I am not sure it was a man."*
*"Miss Eltham, you alarm me. What do you suspect?"*
*"You must think me hysterical and silly, but whilst father*
*and I have been away from Redmoat perhaps the usual*
*precautions have been neglected. Is there any creature, any large*
*creature, which could climb up the wall to the window? Do you*
*know of anything with a long, thin body?"*

—Ibid.

I know a creature, large and long and thin.
It can climb a wall to a window and get in.
It loves neglected rooms. It loves precautions.
It loves suspicious girls with hysterical notions.

It's been away. It's coming back for a spell.
Its body is more alarming than its smell.
(Do you know of anything *that* unusual?)
It's been a silly father, but not a man.
I can't imagine it as well as *you* can.


3
    *"That line of speculation soon takes us out of our depth*
    *Petrie," he said. "Let us stick to what we understand, and that may*
    *help us to a clearer idea of what, at present, is incomprehensible."*

                                          —Ibid.


Sticking to what we understand
Like children trading candy bars
We line up for our bedtime present:
"You're going to get a clearer look
At the incomprehensible,"
He says. "And for a heaping helping
Each will be given an idea
Out of his depth." O Vertigo,
Take us all out of Circulation,
Bring us around to Circumspection,
Deliver us from Speculation.


4
    *"One would expect God's worst man to shrink from employing*
    *—against however vile an enemy—such an instrument as the*
    *Zayat Kiss."*

                                          —Ibid.

Behold this instrument.
It goes *Zayat! Zayat!*
The enemies of God
Shrink when it puckers.
Did you expect, vile man,
Permanent employment
Bussing your worst? Your kiss
Lies smack on the other cheek.


5

*And now the old lady's embarrassment took precedence*
*of her sorrow, and presently the truth came out:*
*"There's a—young lady—in his rooms, sir."*
*I started. This might mean little or might mean much.*

—Ibid


We find, to our embarrassment,
Young ladies leave the room
If the Old observe a precedent
Like calling Love a Shame.

Girls *do* mean little or mean much.
The truth comes out tomorrow.
One touch of nature makes the whole
World kinky, to our sorrow.


6

*"Smith," I said unsteadily, "I have followed your lead*
*blindly in this horrible business and have not pressed for*

*an explanation, but I must insist before I go one step farther*
*upon knowing what it all means."*

—Ibid.

Because of pressing Business As Usual, the blind
Will be unable to lead the blind today.
Instead, the following horrible program
Will be substituted by popular insistence:
One-Step Smith, with his Hammer and Anvil Chorus
Featuring the Broken Eardrums will explain
What everything means if it's inaudible. Go!

*"It's not too much of a dull moment, and I'm not in one place
at one time."*

> —Police recruit on NBC News, stating why he liked
> police work

As a member of the force, you must consider what force
You will use to defend your streets and citizens
To keep them in working order.
You have your hands, nightstick and whistle, and a gun, of course,
But can uphold the law at times by your simple presence,
Implying the power
Structured behind you as solid as penitentiaries
By looking solid and straight and uniform.
You must remember
Complaints are usually the work of the complainers,
And your greatest rewards will come from suspicious persons,
Those who act different,
Who walk too fast or too slow, who avoid your eyes, turn corners
Abruptly and look back, or who ask you silly questions
Over and over
To keep you in one place at a time. You must make them answer
The basic queries of a trade famous for queries—
Who are you? Do you have a license?
Can you walk a straight white line?—But the ambitious patrol-
man prefers
Following in secret. Suppose one climbs a fence,
Crawls into the cellar
Of a deserted factory at midnight and disappears.
Now what do you do? You have suspicions
That law and order
Are being transgressed free of charge. The keeping of the peace

And the protection of property (your luminous guidelines)
Should carry you over
The fence and through the window, regardless of hazards,
After which by following the standard routines
Of search and seizure
You may find him, for instance, boxed in a dark corner,
Looking old and sleepy, proclaiming his innocence.
Officer, officer,
This man begging you of all people to forgive his trespasses
Is guilty of breaking and entering for all intents
And purposes, whether
He meant to achieve a felony or not. Your powers
Do not include the granting of privileges
Or exceptions or
The unofficial establishment of sleeping quarters.
The efficient use of a nightstick as an extension
Of your arm and armor
Lies at the heart of patrolling: each human body
Has tender and vulnerable places whose location,
By trial and error,
You may find to your advantage. This man, being down and out,
Is useless except to demonstrate disorder,
So tie up all loose ends.
The mechanics of arrest require a degree of restraint
Which may consist of inflicting deadly wounds
Or touching a sleeve with a finger:
You may take your choice, depending on circumstances.
It's wiser to be the cause of emergencies
Than their prisoner.
No news is good news. The bulk of your daily labors
Will involve the crisp amusements and temptations

That all men long for,
The action, the power, the pursuit of unhappiness.
Fives, tens, and twenties, up to a half a dozen,
Can be folded over
To the size of a matchbook; but the seemingly drab colors
Are instantly recognizable from a distance.
The trouble, therefore,
Is not in finding adequate compensation, but keeping it
From showing too clearly. The rest is in your hands
As a credit to the force.

# Fortuna Imperatrix Mundi

Lady of the turning numbers, our gaudy wheeler, aloft and
                                                 upstage,
   Come down to us now by every ramp and runway
     At our first sign of distress,
Vagina Dentata Immaculata, Matrix of the Plebian Darkness,
   With tassels whirling clockwise and counterclockwise
     From the peaks of your breasts,
Descend and disrobe, lift up our mouths by the sullen corners
And dazzle us with the blazonry of your sequins,
     Come zipping from the flies,
While all the falling waters sing your praise out of porcelain,
   Come rippling with love, our beautiful grounds for divorce
     With ineluctable thighs,
Our stitch in the side of time. O see, your followers
   Are coming across the patchily-lit, rag-baggedly
     Hunching earth under arches,
Through clumps and bogholes toward you, flying off the handle,
   Rebounding from slumps and falling from the windows of
                                    wallets,
     Redoubled and vulnerable,
They are coming with the jerks of spastics, with congenital
                                     hernias,
   The multitudinous lovers clutching your outskirts,
   The orphans of your storms,
And bearing their jiggers and bitters, the upright citizens,
   Their faces hanging knock-eyed from their skulls,
   Come floating as proud as punch
To lie at your lofty feet. O whirl us in your drums
   Head over heels together like bingo numbers.
   The show must never go on

Without you, our double-breasted starlet, sweet frump of
our days,
Great punchboard we gloss over and prize open
Forever and ever.

## The Middle of Nowhere

To be here, in the first place, is sufficiently amazing:
The flat, tough, gray-green, prickly, star-shaped weeds
Are the sole proprietors
Of a stretch of clay and shale; the cracks zigzagging
Under bleached husks and stems follow directions
Not yet invented—north
By south, upright by easterly, northwest by nothing—
And a cracked rock the size of a cornerstone
Is the only landmark;
The sun is too high, too rigorous, too downright for measuring.
This patch may have a name and co-ordinates
By Sextant out of Star
Or out of Map by Compass, but the problem of being
Here is not deducible—though the eyes,
Nose, tongue, and fingers,
The outer and inner ears may suggest some calculations:
With perfect eyesight, a sense of smell, good taste,
A feeling for surfaces,
Judgment of temperature, and absolute pitch, a balancing
Act of a kind may be carried out against
The odds for a moment,
But the curvature of the earth and the curvature of a spine
Have little connection beyond the geotropism
That keeps one round
And the other upright against its natural habit of lying.
Location is the same as dislocation:
The middle of nowhere
Is portable, reusable, and indispensable. It is something
For nothing, the hole in all the assembled data
Through which we look
Beyond the sags and flaps, the lap-overs and interlockings

Of the usual dimensions into the pit
At the heart of our matter,
Which is neither logical nor ecological, abstaining
As it must from left- and right-handedness,
Bilateral judgment,
And all the makers of haphazard dichotomies under the sun.
This is the place where we must be ready to take
The truths or consequences
Of which there are none to be filched or mastered or depended on,
Not even, as it was in the beginning, the Word
Or, here, the squawk of a magpie.

1

*Then the Lord answered Job out of the whirlwind, and said,*
*Who is this that darkeneth counsel by words without knowledge?*
*Gird up now thy loins like a man; for I will demand of thee,*
*and answer thou me.*

Replying without the benefit of whirlwinds
(A formal answer turneth away wrath)
And, in your honor, leaving my loins alone,
I'll speak as much like a man as anyone
Made in your image can afford to. Sir,
Out of charity, remember, the words of my mouth
Are part of a language you and I contend with
Daily, which nightly darkens, whose darkness ripens.

2

*Where wast thou when I laid the foundations of the earth?*
  *declare, if thou hast understanding.*
*Who hath laid the measures thereof, if thou knowest? or who*
  *hath stretched the line upon it?*
*Whereupon are the foundations thereof fastened? or who*
  *laid the corner stone thereof;*
*When the morning stars sang together, and all the sons of*
  *God shouted for joy?*

Was it with chalk- and plumb-line you held sway?
Master of transits, what did you survey?
Did you forget to check the lens for flaws?
Where in the world did you think the corner was?
What must we do to hear the morning stars
Singing again while day breaks in our ears?
Why do you offer only cornerstones

To those who shout for bread and love?—*our* sons.
The morning stars turn separate and dim.
The evening stars lie far apart and dumb.

3

> *Or who shut up the sea with doors, when it brake forth, as if
> it had issued out of the womb?*
> *When I made the cloud the garment thereof, and thick darkness
> a swaddlingband for it,*
> *And brake up for it my decreed place, and set bars and doors,*
> *And said, Hitherto shalt thou come, but no further: and here
> shall thy proud waves be stayed?*

It has unbarred your doors, risen and fallen,
Swelled, and broken its way
Through our frail houses, crashed, come heaving back
Over thousands of doorsills
Where some lay hopeful, uttering in the wake
Their rite of passage,
Only to vanish in a moony glitter.
It wears our garments
Or yours or the sun's wreckage, coming and going
Not out of pride, like us,
But out of control in the buckles of the wind
And the racking seabed.

4

> *Hast thou commanded the morning since thy days; and caused
> the dayspring to know his place;*
> *That it might take hold of the ends of the earth, that the
> wicked might be shaken out of it?*

*It is turned as clay to the seal; and they stand as a garment.*
*And from the wicked their light is withholden, and the high*
*arm shall be broken.*

If I commanded morning's sagging springs,
I too would shake the earth like a stale blanket,
Hoping to snap the wicked out of it.
But when they rouse, they rise into the light
And flourish and look both prosperous and healthy.
The sun shines on the evil and the holy,
And blessed few have cared where it came from.
*Deposuit potentas?* The lowest arm
Has been broken far more often than the highest.
When they topple, the Mighty fall hard on the Lowly.

5

*Hast thou entered into the springs of the sea? or hast thou*
*walked in the search of the depth?*
*Have the gates of death been opened unto thee? or hast thou*
*seen the doors of the shadow of death?*

Although the primal face
Of the waters seemed your own
(Where you moved and had your way),
It mirrors mine as well.
I have gone spiralling down
Out of my depth, not yours,
And touched the gradual slope
That leads to the abyss,
Your pitch-black charnel house
Where sharks' teeth and the frail

Cupped earbones of great whales
Have fallen through the years,
And there, as I do this day,
I saw the open doors.
They opened long ago
Like my eyes in the night
And haven't yet gone shut
Out of sympathy, out of hope.
I carry their shadow now
Under each scything eyebrow.


6

> Hast thou perceived the breadth of the earth? declare if thou
> knowest it all.
> Where is the way where light dwelleth? and as for darkness,
> where is the place thereof,
> That thou shouldest take it to the bound thereof, and that
> thou shouldest know the paths to the house thereof?
> Knowest thou it, because thou wast then born? or because the
> number of thy days is great?

Unless you count the dizzy curlicues
Of its path in four or five obscure directions,
The breadth of the earth is not quite what it was.
Breadth is a way of feeling. Light is a function
And dwells in its own process, goes where it must,
Comes back impartially for better or worse,
For richer or poorer from what interferes,
And darkness is only the other side of that
Or the next dull inch beyond its dimmest outpost.
I know the way to that house: it's down and in.

I know that now because I was born, because
I'm old enough not to know better. What I know
Has come from dark and light: the missed, the imagined,
The uncreated and the created motion
That lies in my mouth and the mouths of erring stars.


7

*Hast thou entered into the treasures of the snow? or hast
thou seen the treasures of the hail,
Which I have reserved against the time of trouble, against the
day of battle and war?*

Is that cold storage all your wrath?
Snowbanks and hailstones all your wealth?
I know a fire to melt them both.
Where shall we play in such foul weather?


8

*By what way is the light parted, which scattereth the east
wind upon the earth?
Who hath divided a watercourse for the overflowing of waters,
or a way for the lightning of thunder;
To cause it to rain on the earth, where no man is; on the
wilderness, wherein there is no man;
To satisfy the desolate and waste ground; and to cause the bud
of the tender herb to spring forth?*

We turn away from the light each day to breathe
The cooler air that lies in our own shade:

This is the way: a curve from north to south,
Thanks to the Primum Mobile who made
This ball of dust and water wobble eastward.

If rain should fall on the waste land and lift out
The sage from the cracked rock for a little season,
Why not more rain for every wilderness?
Meanwhile, we dig our ditches by the sweat
Of our furrowed brows and rake the bare horizon.


9

*Hath the rain a father? or who hath begotten the drops of dew?*
*Out of whose womb came the ice? and the hoary frost of heaven,*
*    who hath gendered it?*
*The waters are hid as with a stone, and the face of the deep*
*    is frozen.*

Old Water Carrier, gray Cloudy Father,
Only Begetter of Dew,
Calver of Glaciers, blue-thumbed Iceberg-Maker,
Dumfounder of Zero,
No one can doubt your solid achievements,
But you look frozen.
Lie down with us and warm your hands at our hearts
From the frostbite of Heaven.


10

*Canst thou bind the sweet influences of Pleiades, or loose*
*    the bands of Orion?*

*Canst thou bring forth Mazzaroth in his season? or canst thou*
*guide Arcturus with his sons?*
*Knowest thou the ordinances of heaven? canst thou set the*
*dominion thereof in the earth?*

The Pleiades ride the shoulder of the Bull;
Their sweetness now is problematical.

Orion hunts for Mazzaroth in the dark;
Neither can hear the summons back to work.

Arcturus, with the Herdsman, chases bears
With dogs, not sons, across the bent light-years.

Their seasons go: Red Giant, large and light,
Through yellow to blue, then Pale Dwarf, then goodnight.

The heavens shift and redden at the loss.
Dominion is as a Dominion does.

11

*Canst thou lift up thy voice to the clouds, that abundance of*
*waters may cover thee?*
*Canst thou send lightnings, that they may go, and say unto thee,*
*Here we are?*

We lift or lower our voices, rain or shine,
Drink in the sun or whisper under water,
And lightning strikes both ways, now up, now down,
Behaving handsomely in each direction.
The weather serves us best in conversation.
(We have more difficult servants than the weather.)

**12**

*Who hath put wisdom in the inward parts? or who hath given*
*understanding to the heart?*

If we have wisdom in our parts,
Why do they act like idiots
Muttering solos at the moon?
Shall our lungs inspire us? Shall the spleen
Edge out the errors of our wits?
Does the right pathway lie through giblets?
Is all our sorrow lack of gall?
*Our* understanding is: hearts fail.


**13**

*Who can number the clouds in wisdom? or who can stay the*
*bottles of heaven,*
*When the dust groweth into hardness, and the clods cleave*
*fast together?*

Our wisdom is as cloudy as it was
Before we learned to count the numberless.

We take our bottles, hellish or heavenly,
From either shelf and cork them once a day.

And every clod turns over once a year
To raise its dust a brief while in the air.

**14**

*Wilt thou hunt the prey for the lion? or fill the appetite of the*
*young lions . . . ?*
*Who provideth for the raven his food? When his young ones*
*cry unto God . . . ?*
*Who hath sent out the wild ass free? or who hath loosed*
*the bands of the wild ass? . . .*
*Will the unicorn be willing to serve thee, or abide by thy crib? . . .*
*Gavest thou the goodly wings unto the peacocks? or wings and*
*feathers unto the ostrich? . . .*
*Hast thou given the horse strength? hast thou clothed his*
*neck with thunder? . . .*
*Doth the hawk fly by thy wisdom, and stretch her wings toward*
*the south?*
*Doth the eagle mount up at thy command, and make her*
*nest on high?*

Lions and ravens hunger for just cause:
What fills their mouths with dust is not *their* claws.
The goats kneel down in April; the wild ass
Goes far afield to hide from what he knows.
Left to itself, the lovely unicorn
Impales the poet's mind where it was born.
The peacock struts and screams. The ostrich runs
Against the God that nested her on stones.
Which is more terrible: the frightened horse
Or the dead charger's hamstrung swollen carcass?
The hawk and eagle build commanding thrones,
Perch for a while, then cross their bones on bones.
Stabbed in the deep or shot under the sun,
Behemoth shrivels, and Leviathan.

My dust will settle. Its crime was to presume
To suffer more than the next man and to blame
You, in your whirlwind, not its bitter self,
To have reviled its measure of this life.
Now it shall empty, grain by grain, its cup
In sleep for sleep through sleep to sleep past sleep.

Stretched out on the ground, I hear the news of the night
Pass over and under:
The faraway honks of geese flying blind as stars
(And hoof- or heartbeats),
The squeaks of bats, impaling moths in the air,
Who leave light wings
To flutter by themselves down to the grass
(And under that grass
The thud and thump of meeting, the weasel's whisper),
Through the crackling thorns
Over creekbeds up the ridge and against the moon,
The coyotes howling
All national anthems, cresting, picking up
Where men leave off
(And, beneath, the rumble of faulted and flawed earth
Shaking its answer).

## Waiting with the Snowy Owls

Their yellow eyes as blank as the end
Of winter under the chickenwire,
Nine snowy owls are waiting.

They stand on the ground and stare at anything
Moving, their leg-tufts drifting
Like snow over their talons.

They came south like the snow, when winter hardened
Behind them, to be met by the shots and shouts
Of all our finders and keepers.

Now they wait under the sun for it to melt
What holds them, to run from them or stir
The thawed halves of hearts at their feet.

They stare through the mesh at the green welter
Of spring in the children's zoo. I wait
On the walk beside them, unable to read or write.

# To Be Sung on the Water

*for Rolfe Humphries, 1894–1969*

Whatever you say or sing
On the water should be fading.
The air has far to go
After it leaves you,
Rising and falling down
To the sea like the weather.
You needn't sing at all
If, when you hold still,
The wavering of the wind
Against you, against you
Is simpler and more telling.
Listen, and end now
Moved only by the water.

# Halcyon Days

*for James Wright*

Remember the day we went to Halcyon
To see the poet? The thick front door was locked
And the door at the top of the stairway, but his door
Had a hole for a doorknob, mesh for a window.
We sat. He smoked a cigar for us, rehearsing
Or reenacting Hell for our benefit—
Two former students who racked their brains for him,
Who went there sober and came away as drunk
As judges, refusing sentence after sentence.

They've taken the place apart, yanked off the roof,
Scrapped all the tubs and beaten the walls out.
The Violent Ward, including the Rec Room,
Has wound up upside down in the driveway
Without permission, and chunks of linoleum
Lie strewn on the slope like manic steppingstones.
They're levelling it and the bluff with a bulldozer,
Smoothing everything out. It's visitors' day
All day and all night from this day forward.
*Here lay one whose nest was built on water.*

# Elegy for the Nondescript

"The matamata, Chelus fimbriata, a South American turtle,
is not alone remarkable in having a long, laterally folding
neck. It is one of Nature's nondescripts, standing in a genus
by itself."

—Raymond L. Ditmars, *Reptiles of the World*

He looked like something wrecked or broken, a mistake uncovered
To no good purpose from under the roots and disembodied matter
Of marshes. Even by daylight he looked like nothing
Between the sun and the moon. In his plastic pool, under the red
  lamp
Like a developing negative, he waited all day and night
To do what he was made for: to eat whatever wandered into range
Of his foot-long, lunging neck and the wide pink maw
Undercutting his tiny snout. As big as a roast platter
And as thick as a roast, he lived in our basement for a year,
Snapping thawed smelt that shook at the end of tongs.

Picked up by the sides, he made a dripping armload, his plastron
Like a phalanx of soaked sticks, the skin of his head
And forelegs scalloped like leaves, the huge neck snaking
Around as thick as the wrists that held it, looking lethal.
Now to the catalogue of our lives and deaths we add to our sorrow
This undistinguishable matamata who choked on his dinner,
  having bitten off
(Like us in keeping him) more than he could chew,
The past and present master of holding still, of not being
Seen or heard, the essence of a gulp being gulped back into
  essence,
Who scared us out of our uncertain wits and into his.

We found the salmon on its side, the river no longer
Covering all of it, the hooked jaws gaping
And closing around as much sharp air as water.

It lay on the stones, far from the nesting hollow,
Its dark flanks battered cadaver-white, and fungus
Scaling its gills the color of marigolds.

"Help it," she said. "I can't help it, it's dying"—
Looking hard at the upper eye struck dull
As a stone, overcast with cataracts.

But it splashed to life, came scuttering, fishtailing forward
As if the two of us were a place upstream,
And we saw its humpback writhe ashore, then tilt

Upright in an inch of water. It mouthed the ripples
And stared with both eyes now at the empty sunlight,
Not knowing where it was. I turned it away

With my boot, catching my breath. It lurched and slid
To a pool as deep as its body, then lunged in the current
And gradually fell downstream, while we followed it

(Where the yellow leaves came scattering to the shallows)
And watched its dorsal fin be joined by another
To hang there, wavering, for the cold time being.

The rain is pummelling
Our hemlock again and again,
And slapdash lightning knocks
The daylight out of the sky.
My love, what passes
For air in a cloudburst comes
Through all the baffling branches,
Lifting dust to the light,
To the disembodied wind
And water around us
Like the chaos and old night
We spilled out of these hearts
To make our firmament.

Quivering through the field
Like the stubble of the night,
The first straw-colored light
Touches our windowsill.
Real straw lies in the stable.
Real wheat lies under stone.
Whenever we lie down,
My love, we turn together
Toward the edge of dawn
And fall for the thousandth time
Under the sweeping scythe
That levels all we have
To keep under the sun.

# A Morning on the Outside

Arizona looked like this: beyond the saguaros
The graveyard spilled like a landslide
From cairn to cairn and down to the newly dead
In clay the color of good Pápago Indians.
By the whitewashed cross we stood above it all,
Then tried the crooked path, expecting each foot
To touch a diamondback
As we went down to the ground like the dead before us.

Close up, each grave was a rubble
Of plastic flowers and kitchenware and beercans
(Unpunctured, for the Land of the Dead) and tracks
Of animals. And the nearest chest-high cairn
Had had a stone pulled inward like a gunport
Out of which nothing looked. Near the end
Of the line, a two-foot barrel cactus,
Kicked over and left for dead, was turning blue
As a drowned man. At the foot of the newest grave,
A fresh-dug burrow big enough for a dog
Led down and inward. The woman I believe in
Reached among rocks and lifted a shed snakeskin.

At the base of every mesquite and razor bush,
A two-inch burrow sank into the dark
Where the parching roots held on for their own lives.
Behind us, up the next steep crumbling outcrop
At the mouths of caves, the petroglyphs held on
Like us: stick-men and -women scratched on surfaces,
Floating on stone, not at the heart of it.

The wind had snapped the snakeskin in three parts
And the rattle was missing: the outside can't hold on
To itself by itself, and at the latest grave
Something, having found the roots of a man,
Was lying doggo in a nest of ribs.
We stood our ground for a while, then went away,
Held up by sticks for one more desert morning.

Already imagining her
Unwrapping it, I fold the corners,
Putting paper and ribbon between her
And this small box. I could hand it over
Out in the open: why bother to catch her eye
With floss and glitter?
Looking manhandled, it lies there
Like something lost in the mail, the bow
On backwards. And minutes from now,
She will have seen what it is.
But between her guesswork
And the lifting of the lid, I can delay
All disappointments: the give and take
Of love is in the immediate present
Again, though I can't remember myself
What's in it for her.

I swear by the bottomless pit of my stomach,
I had no head for heights.
But stairways and elevators
Were meant for sinking fingernail-filing clerks
And rising janitors,
Not for a rank outsider. When the gargoyles vanished
And the caryatids with their lofty bosoms,
I found something else to cling to
In spite of the architects:
Not the snouts of air-conditioners
Or the ankles of swash-buckling window-washers,
But myself: I stick to what I am.
When I let go, I'll break to thousands of eyes.

# The Vacation

The Indian asked me, "How come you're not working?"
He had on jeans and most of a shirt, one shoe and a Stetson.

I said I was on vacation. He picked up the word
And muttered it, trying it on himself. It didn't fit.

"That means you save up in the winter," he said,
"Then spend it?" Yes, I told him it was something like that.

We stood for a minute looking at half of Montana:
A prairie stretching past a jail and a junkyard

Where the sheep and coyotes both get stiff on the weather
Or poisoned baits, where a vulture can't make a living,

And nobody counts much, with or without a treaty.
He said, "I saved up thirty-nine years, that's all I got,

The years. You got to build a vacation like a house,
One brick at a time." I said I didn't doubt it.

"We're supposed to save up summer for the winter,"
He said, "but look at how hot. It bakes the dirt

Like bricks. If I had a brick, I'd drink it."
I gave him the price of a brick, and he took it.

And he went back to work at saving up years
For all the good it would do him. I was no help.

And that was my vacation: I vacated a house
And went to a vacant place palmed off on the Indians

For recreation, in order to recreate, supposedly,
A self worth carrying in this hod on my shoulders.

That end of Montana is still the end of Montana.
This is my work, and this is the end of it.

## Do Not Proceed Beyond This Point Without a Guide

The official warning, nailed to a hemlock,
Doesn't say why. I stand with my back to it,
Afraid I've come as far as I can
By being stubborn, and look
Downward for miles at the hazy crags and spurs.

A rubble-covered ridge like a bombed stairway
Leads up beyond the sign. It doesn't
Seem any worse than what I've climbed already.
Why should I have to take a guide along
To watch me scaring myself to death?

What was it I wanted? A chance to look around
On a high rock already named and numbered
By somebody else? A chance to shout
Over the heads of people who quit sooner?
Shout what? I can't go tell it on the mountain.

I sit for a while, raking the dead leaves
Out of my lungs and travelling light-headed
Downward again in my mind's eye, till there's nothing
Left on my feet but rags and bones
And nothing to look down on but my shoes.

The closer I come to it, the harder it is to doubt
How well this mountain can take me or leave me.
The hemlock had more sense. It stayed where it was,
Grew up and down at the same time, branch and root,
Being a guide instead of needing one.

To walk downhill you must lean partially backwards,
Heels digging in,
While your body gets more help than it can use
In following directions—
Because it's possible simply to fall down
The way you're going
Instead of climbing against it. The baffling dead-ends
Of travelling upward
Are turned around now, their openings leading down
To the land you promised
Yourself, beyond box canyons and blind-draws.
They branch repeatedly,
But the direction you choose should be as easy to take
As your right hand.
The sky is a constant; even its variables
Like cirrus and cumulus
Will cancel each other out in a rough balance,
Taking turns at weather.
The wind may bluff and bluster and cut corners
Or skip a whole valley,
But eventually it has nothing to do with you,
Not even when it throws
The dust of your own country in your eyes.
At dawn, at darkness,
The sun will be here or there, full-face, rear-view;
It evens out in the end.
You must keep your goal in mind as clear as day
Though it doesn't matter
What you may think it looks like: second-sight
Is simply perseverance;
And getting there from here is a set of stages

Demanding candle-power,
Foot-pounds and simple levers, thirst and hunger.
Signposts are seasonal
And not forensic: one end may come to a point
And the other be indented,
But the words will be gone, and the rusty earth and air
Will have eaten the pole and nails.
You must take time to notice what grows on rocks
Or squeezes between them—
The gnawing lichen, bone-weed and thorny scrub—
All hanging tough
And gnarling for elbow room or squatters' rights.
These are the straighteners,
The levellers at work on the thick and crooked:
Some distant species
Will find the world made flat by the likes of these.
You must do your bit
By scuffing downhill heel-first on behalf of erosion,
For the sake of another time
When the mountains are made plain and anyone standing
Can see from here to there
Without half-trying. When your shoes are out of step
And your clothes are a burden
And you feel bone-tired, sit down and look around.
You're there. No matter what
You had in mind as a proper circumstance,
You've come to it at last:
A rock-strewn slope from which you have a view
Of a further rock-strewn slope.

You can pick up dust in your hand and let it fall.
The place is real.
You can bite a grass-stem, look, take a deep breath
And, naturally, let it go.

*Do your own time*, say prisoners
To those who spill their lives to others.
I serve my indeterminate years
Through these concurrent sentences
Out of a hope to get time off
For good behavior, doing life
For willful failure to report
On what goes on and on in the heart.

# The First Law of Motion

"*Every body perseveres in its state of rest, or of uniform motion in a right line, unless it is compelled to change that state by forces impressed thereon.*"

—Isaac Newton, *Principia Mathematica*

Staying strictly in line and going
Along with a gag or swinging
Far out and back or simply wheeling
Into the home-stretch again and again,
Not shoving or stalling, but coasting
And playing it smooth, pretending
To make light of it, you can seem
To be keeping it up forever, needing
Little or nothing but your own
Dead weight to meet
The demands of momentum,
But there's no way out of touching
Something or being touched, and like it
Or not, you're going to be
Slowing down because turning
A corner means coming to a dead
Halt, however slight, to change direction,
And your impulse to get moving
Again may never move you, so keeping time
Is as inhuman as the strict first law
Of motion, and going off on your own
On some lopsided jagged course
For which there's no equation, some unbecoming
Switchbacked crossfooted trek in a maze

Of your own invention, some dying
Fall no star could fix, is a state of being
Human at least, and so, at last, is stopping.

The Professor sawed her in half and put her back
Together; chopped off her head, restored it; sat her
Down in a box and thrust long dozens of swords
Through where she was, then brought her out unharmed.
And now he waves her into a final trance
And rests her on a table under a sheet
As white as any lady in a morgue.
She rises smoothly into the spotlit air
And hovers there to music, floating on nothing.

He stands underneath, commanding her to move
Sideways or forward, and she does. He slides
A hoop around her. Isn't she beautiful
Under the sheet where none of us can see her?
Here in the balcony, floating even higher
Than she, we put ourselves in her position,
Lying beside her, trying to weigh her down
To a world of unsliced bodies and mattresses
Where we might love her heavily forever.

But now the Professor yanks the cloth away,
And she's gone. She has disappeared like all her wounds
From crosscut saw and guillotine and sword
And doesn't come back. The Professor takes applause
Like a man saying Q.E.D. to a piece of logic
On a bare stage with the empty sheet in his arms.

We sit at the top of the Pyramid of the Magician
Our last day in Uxmal, afraid
Of the sheer steps and the ranks of the rain gods,
The rows of Chacmuls in stone with their high-flung, fanfaring
    noses.
Having guided ourselves this far, we look
At the ruined ball-court and, beyond, the iguanas basking
In the cracked fretwork of the Palace of the Governor,
The stone jaguars mating in the plaza
By the broken phallus, and with its jammed perspective, the
    quadrangle
Where four classes of priests took charge of the rain.

Not even the Governors were allowed this high to lord it
Over the land from the mouth of the temple
Whose intricate façade is a Chacmul's face
Behind our backs. Not daring to ask for a change in the deep sky,
We wait for our lives to topple
Like the rest, though our hands hold us together, balancing
Our love against the weight of evidence
That has caved in one whole side of this pyramid.

We are masters of nothing we survey,
But what the Magician did from here—chant with his arms
    outstretched
Over a dying city or reach halfway to the clouds sailing aloof
Over the maize fields—is ours to try, since we believe in magic,
Believe we can climb to it slowly, being frightened,
That it can break suddenly out of stone or out of the dry air.
As priest and priestess of ourselves, before praying for rain,
We weep to show it how.

## The Doves of Mérida

We took ourselves to market in Mérida,
Shopping and being shopped
Under the iron roof where, steaming like frijoles,
We were caught up short
After the hammocks and sandals in the long aisles
To find our eyes full of birds:
They sat in cages, jammed in each other's rafters,
The cardinals and honey creepers,
The grackles and finches—and there lay the mourning doves
Huddled together,
Their powdery-rose and mother-of-pearl necks
Twisting out of fear.
Ten pesos per dove, said the *hombre de rapiña,*
The only bargainer
In all of the Yucatan who wouldn't bargain:
A fixed corona of silver
For each, as sure as the price of a medal in the Cathedral
Or a bottle of clear water.
We carried five in a cage through the choking streets,
*Dos gringos locos,*
And plied them with cracked heads of the god of maize,
With water in ashtrays
On the terrace of the hotel. They ate and drank,
Watching life sideways
In the sunlight shrinking back to the Gulf's belly.
We opened their door
And hoped for peace, for land after the flood,
Or hoped for hope.

The first one flew with matted, rump-sprung tailfeathers
High among shade trees

To hold all night in the wind from Cozumel,
To wait for sunrise
And the school of his masters in the Plaza de la Independencia:
The lean gray city pigeons.
The second flew two walls and houses away
To land among turkeys
And chickens as small as he in the rock-strewn courtyard
To peck, in order, at dirt
And fatten himself as a squab for his destiny.
The third one rose
As high as the green caryatids at the roof of the Palacio
De Avis Rent-a-Car,
Then fell to be done to a turn in the sunny gutter,
Drawing the vultures down
In the morning to break their fast. And the fourth,
Heart-forward and swift,
Flew past the tortoiseshell shop of Sr. Carrillo Gonzalez
Where the stuffed turtles
Pluck their guitars in rows as if mourning their shells,
Over vendors wearing skulls
And over the barking dogs in the butcher's attic
And the zippered armadillos,
Not touching the broken glass on the tops of the walls
Around the dense gardens
Of the descendants of Don Francisco de Montejo—the Conqueror,
The dismantler of the gods—
As sweet and close as pyramids of fruit salad.
It skimmed past the zoo
And the *barrios* where adobe, heaped up like sandbags,
Looked something like houses,
And past the Aeropuerto, high over the highway

And the heaped-up burros
Where the thatched huts crackle and shrink in the day's oven
And the children shrink from the doors
And the stucco drops from the empty bell-towers of churches,
Flew over gigantic rows
Of sisal patched against jungle rooted in ruins,
Past the rubble of cities
And over the iguanas shaking their fringed jowls
At the last of the light,
And flew before dark to the gray-green hummocks of Uxmal
Past the steep empty stairs
Of the Pyramid of the Magician. At the broken Casa de las
    Palomas
It flapped to its rest
Where the Mayans left holes in stone for the singing wind,
The maker of doves and rain.

And the fifth one circled upward, groping for distance,
Turning half gold,
And disappeared before our eyes could tell it apart
From what was beyond it.
We gave the empty cage, for what it was worth,
To a straight-faced waiter,
Then flew away, flew far in the dead of night
To our own fortunes.

# The Gathering of the Loons

In the dead calm before darkness near the shore
The loons are gathering, rippling blue-gray
As slow as driftwood, the lighthouse blinking
And sweeping across the long calls of the gulls,
The scoters darkening, the breathlessly sighing
Wingbeats of goldeneyes across the marshgrass
Lifting the widgeons up in gold-streaked wedges
To take one way toward night against the mountains,
And the still loons, the solitary loons
Drifting together out into the bay,
The silent loons all floating toward sleep.

Young men, not knowing what to remember,
Come to this hiding place of the moons and years,
To this Old Man. Old Man, they say, where should we go?
Where did you find what you remember? Was it perched in a tree?
Did it hover deep in the white water? Was it covered over
With dead stalks in the grass? Will we taste it
If our mouths have long lain empty?
Will we feel it between our eyes if we face the wind
All night, and turn the color of earth?
If we lie down in the rain, can we remember sunlight?

He answers, I have become the best and worst I dreamed.
When I move my feet, the ground moves under them.
When I lie down, I fit the earth too well.
Stones long under water will burst in the fire, but stones
Long in the sun and under the dry night
Will ring when you strike them. Or break in two.
There were always many places to beg for answers:
Now the places themselves have come in close to be told.
I have called even my voice in close to whisper with it:
Every secret is as near as your fingers.
If your heart stutters with pain and hope,
Bend forward over it like a man at a small campfire.

Stand still. The trees ahead and bushes beside you
Are not lost. Wherever you are is called Here,
And you must treat it as a powerful stranger,
Must ask permission to know it and be known.
The forest breathes. Listen. It answers,
I have made this place around you.
If you leave it, you may come back again, saying Here.
No two trees are the same to Raven.
No two branches are the same to Wren.
If what a tree or a bush does is lost on you,
You are surely lost. Stand still. The forest knows
Where you are. You must let it find you.

Though your brothers, after the long hunt and the fasting,
After holding still, have found Fox, Bear Mother,
Or Snake at their sides and taken them
Into the empty mouths of their spirits,
Do not be jealous. They will be cunning
Or strong or good at dreaming. Do not be ashamed
That you—when the day changed, when the first hour
Came falling suddenly over the last hour—
Found only Fog as the eye of your heart opened.

Now when your feet touch earth, nothing will know you.
You will move without moving a leaf,
Climb the steep cliffside as easily as Hawk,
Cross water, pass silently as Owl.
You will become trees by holding them inside you,
And tall stones, become a whole valley
Where birds fall still, where men stay close to fires.
You without wings or hands will gleam against them,
They will breathe you, they will be lost in you,
Your song will be the silence between their songs,
Your white darkness will teach them,
You will wrap all love and fear in a beautiful blindness.